How Progressivism Destroyed Venezuela

A Cautionary Tale

Elizabeth Rogliani

How Progressivism
Destroyed Venezuela

A Cautionary Tale

GAUDIUM

Gaudium Publishing

Las Vegas ◊ Oxford ◊ Palm Beach

Published in the United States of America by
Histria Books, a division of Histria LLC
7181 N. Hualapai Way, Ste. 130-86
Las Vegas, NV 89166 USA
HistriaBooks.com

Gaudium Publishing is an imprint of Histria Books. Titles published under the imprints of Histria Books are distributed worldwide.

Library of Congress Control Number: 2021940155

ISBN 978-1-59211-134-3 (hardcover)

Contents

Introduction

It's certainly strange to think that one decision can change the course of a nation. One decision, one day, one battle, one vote. Just one key thing can take what once was and turn it into something completely different, either for better or worse.

But that one thing is also the result of many other things that people often ignore. People let them pass by as they attribute little to no importance to them.

What if they change this one rule? What if the demographic composition of the country radically changes? Or, what if, in the name of progress, we let go of those moral principles that set up the foundation of the country? Those are changes that are invisible to most people living day to day, but they are critical. A trap. A slippery slope.

Venezuela became what it is today, a failed state, by many such seemingly innocuous changes. And then, finally, the vote that put the nail in the coffin.

I grew up during the time of the acceleration to the disaster that is now my country, during its downward spiral. And even in those times, a new kind of complacency sets in. While year by year, more freedoms are taken away.

Humans are very adaptable creatures. A new "normal" can set in every few months. There is nothing that proves that better than the year 2020, where people willingly gave away their rights and their neighbor's rights in the name of "safety." But the idea of safety is a trap.

In two decades, Venezuela has gone through a massive political, socio-economic, and ideological transformation, from a stable democracy in Latin America where people wanted to immigrate to a failed state with an enormous brain drain.

I wrote this book intending to explore what happened, both before we took this path as a nation and after the course was set in motion in 1998. I wrote it to lead myself and the reader through the defining moments of the so-called "progressive" leadership in Venezuela. Through the policies, events, and attitudes that have defined the last 20 years of Venezuela. And how that utterly failed leadership still manages to cement itself in the country, which half a century earlier would have rejected it with all its strength.

How a population that was well on its way to first-world status threw it all away with a single vote. And how liberties, once taken for granted, were taken away one by one.

I

Planting the Seeds

In 1808, Napoleon Bonaparte occupied Spain and named his younger brother, Joseph Bonaparte, King of Spain. Only two years later, members of the Caracas oligarchy, those known as "criollos" (Spaniards born in the Venezuelan province), got together to discuss the new taxes which they paid regularly to Spain. The "criollos" were not very keen on the new taxes imposed on the provinces, which required them to pay taxes to France on top of those they paid to the Spanish crown. They decided that they would keep paying the regular taxes to Spain, but refused to pay new ones to France or for the reconstruction of Spain. Spanish America did not recognize the rule of Joseph Bonaparte. Of course, this unleashed a conflict which eventually led the Venezuelan province to declare itself independent from Spain, and shortly thereafter, before the return of the legitimate King of Spain, a brutal War of Independence began on the new continent, which would last ten years in Venezuela, and would decimate half of the Europeans living on Venezuelan soil.

Venezuela's early founders had a deep appreciation for European culture and its way of life. They held the firm belief that it was through those cultural ideals that the new nation had to be constructed. Simón Bolívar had led a brutal war against the Spanish Empire and eventually led the way for the independence and annexation of Colombia, Panama, Ecuador, and Guyana, into what was briefly to be known as one single country: La Gran Colombia (or Greater Colombia). Soon after the creation of Greater Colombia, companies were formed to recruit, relocate, and place European immigrants in the new continent. The founders put great emphasis on immigrants from Great Britain, the Netherlands, France, Germany, and Denmark.

The vision the early Venezuelan patriots had for our country was one of European liberal values of enlightenment and libertarianism. Flash forward from then to 2020, it is obvious just how far we have departed from those dreams. Consider a speech made in the early 1800s, about the concept they held for the nation:

> Imagine for a moment Venezuela united and animated by the spirit of enterprise, marching along the new route that patriotism opens, and you will see the abundance placed in public works, to clean the ports, create the docks, build aqueducts, dry up the swamps, dig channels, pave roads, establish banks, open bazaars, form walks, illuminate streets, you will see the treasure of wisdom, deposited in the talent of individuals, consecrated to the company of spreading the knowledge in normal schools

and in public courses in agriculture, chemistry, botany; and to apply, finally, scientific principles to useful and necessary arts, and to remove from our education the fatal taste for metaphysical subtleties, or unrealizable theories with which we recharge our heads to leave tactless the hands destined to handle public affairs, or to work in the fields and in the arts...

By their early words, they seem to have a disdain for what we today call the liberal arts, which many students in my generation study to fill their heads with nothing but relativistic ideas, and with barely any practical skills to apply to society; such as gender studies.

Let us, then, inflame our patriotism, unite our faculties, and we will lack nothing, without laws or decrees we will do everything, the treasury will need less income, and the administration will find itself freer to contract its essential attributions: to watch over common order and security.

It is evident by these words that they envisioned a Venezuela that was to have a self-reliant population. A population that would keep most of what they earned, and a government with a small budget that served merely to protect the fundamental rights of freedom and the life of the nation's citizens. It was important for this newly-established land to educate its citizens with useful and productive activities. To promote prosperity and wellness, they had to incentivize productivity, abandon the practice of expecting the government to take care of its citizens, and abandon the practice of citizens depending on their governments.

Although these visions for Venezuela are important to note, it is equally important to observe how Venezuela's government was organized, even if it is a more tedious part of the story. In the terms established in the Constitution of the Republic (or the Carta Magna), Venezuela assumed the form of a decentralized state. The national territory was divided into states, a capital district, federal agencies, and federal territories. The states would also be divided into municipalities. Similarly, the public distribution of power was divided between the state government, the national government, and municipal governments, each with their own authority. The Venezuelan state was divided by the Constitution into five different branches: the legislative branch, the executive branch, the judicial branch, the citizen's branch, and the electoral branch. Each of these branches had its own functions, but the government bodies that formed these branches were meant to collaborate to carry out the state's goals. Therefore, even though independent, they were each a cog in a wheel. One thing that changed in our recent history was the legislative branch, which used to be two chambers in Congress: the Senate and the House. However, as of 1999, the two-chamber system was dissolved and what remained was the National Assembly, the sole legislative body. There is still hope amongst present-day opposition members that one day we can restore the two-chamber system.

Despite all the human potential of Venezuela, our natural resources, and key geographic position, the country was subject to a cluster of ideas that favored Utopian dreams where the concept of private property does not exist. In other words, there is no such thing as, "what is yours is yours, and what is mine is mine." Venezuelan academia adopted these ideas early on. These ideas gained favored as Venezuela saw a gradual growth of government, which gradually started to eliminate the country's early visions. To this day, the groups who pushed for what Venezuela became have not taken responsibility for their part in the disaster. The politicians, the professors, the judges, the prosecutors, the teachers, etc., were all largely to blame for the nation's moral and institutional decay. But the decline happened so gradually that most of the population barely noticed. For the political elites, it was beneficial for them in the short term to enact specific changes that affected society through endless price controls, confiscation, nationalization, and the slow suspension of economic freedom. This was done little by little — not enough for the people to notice the wrong turn the country had taken. In fact, through the nineteenth and twentieth centuries, Venezuela experienced favorable immigration from European nations, and even a small German colony was established near the capital. Half of my family arrived in Venezuela in the nineteenth century to Rio Caribe, a fishing region mostly made up of immigrants from Spain and Italy. This was a new nation. Even though the seeds for its decay were already being planted, the new settlers' entrepreneurial spirit almost made the effects of these seeds invisible, even though voices were warning the politicians of imminent destruction. It shouldn't surprise us that Venezuela went through a series of right-wing military dictatorships in the twentieth century, trying to correct the course of left-wing politicians who had squandered the national budget.

There were liberal ideas that were important in shaping the first formal constitutional essays and, therefore, the foundations of Venezuela and even other Latin American countries. These liberal rationalist ideas were contaminated by the repudiation of religious norms, the norms of courtesy, and any moral tradition that could not be rationally justified. It's as if they ignored the key aspect of the societies they appreciated: the foundation rooted in Christian values and objective morality. The writing of the constitutional essays and the creation of Venezuela as a modern society was going to serve as an instrument of social transformation that was meant to guarantee individual freedoms and "social justice" ideas that were going to oppose the freedoms of the individual and the small government but would contribute to the notion of "collectivism."

I realize today it is hard to imagine this country, a Venezuela that used to be a bastion of ideas and strong leadership, leading to emancipation. However, it is true that despite all these Venezuelan ideas that contributed to the independence of other South American nations, they still were not quite as well-formed as those that the founding fathers forged for the United States, our northern neighbor. The question is: why? One theory is that, unlike what happened in the United States, Spanish America did not place as much significance on ideas such as federalism, the separation of powers, and the role of the president. Yes, the ideas were undoubtedly there, but they had simply not been culturally present in the time of colonial Spain; therefore, their importance to the newly independent Venezuelan nation was of a lesser degree. Some say, however, that perhaps the Venezuelan Constitution allowed for too much political freedom, which meant the basis of the destruction of those same freedoms.

The Twentieth Century

We have reached the point where many readers may be wondering if I am going to blame the decay of modern Venezuela on its early beginnings and mistakes or on Hugo Chávez Frías. The answer is: I blame both. Chávez merely put his foot on the accelerator. However, the early seeds still permitted Venezuela to function as a society where people were content, and there was perhaps a hope of prosperity and building a future for your family. Chávez erased that. Let us further examine what paved the way for Hugo Chávez Frias to install a system for the complete destruction of the vision of the early founders, the "criollos."

Let's jump back for a moment to one of the key struggles between the left and the right in mid-twentieth century Venezuela. In the early 1940s, Venezuela was governed by General Isaías Medina Angarita, whom many agree was one of Venezuela's best presidents. General Angarita, however, despite being a member of the military, was considering eliminating the Venezuelan military forces, which brought anger and resentment from career military men. This anger, seeded in the minds of career military men, was met by the ambitious Rómulo Betancourt, a career politician who intended to re-direct Venezuela towards the left. He used that military anger to his advantage — he deposed Angarita from office in 1945 and installed a new government with a civilian-military junta led by himself. Betancourt led with a quasi-communist, ultra-leftist leaning government. During the three years he was in office, he transformed the voting system from a tier system to a direct popular vote. Prior to this voting reform, voters would elect representatives for the legislative House of Congress of their own state and their council members. These local representatives would then select the senators and congressmen of the two chambers of Congress. Finally, both houses would then pick the president in what was known as the "United States of Venezuela." While President Betancourt led the nation during those three years, there was a war against private education, a raise in taxes imposed on the oil industry, and an attack against the Church (a common theme of leftist governments, it seems). While Betancourt may have used the armed forces against General Medina, he also recognized that the same military could end his leftist government. Therefore, he started instituting a system of propaganda throughout the nation, designed to instill in the minds of the public that the men in uniform were "the bad guys."

Eventually, however, he wasn't successful, and it was, in fact, the military that ended his government in 1948. They again created a civilian-military junta led by Carlos Delgado Chalbaud. After Betancourt was removed, there was a period of economic progress, national prosperity, and peace. However, in 1950, Carlos

Delgado Chalbaud was kidnapped and assassinated in a leftist coup attempt. However, the coup against the right-wing leadership failed, because immediately after his death, a new junta was created by the military which was led by civilian Germán Suárez Flamerich, General Marcos Evangelista Pérez Jiménez, and Lieutenant Colonel Luis Felipe Llovera Páez. They governed this way for two years until elections were held in 1952, where Marcos Pérez Jiménez was installed as the new president. Pérez Jiménez emphasized and incentivized European immigration, specifically Portuguese, Italian, and Spanish, to promote social cohesion and assimilation. His leadership and sound social and economic policies garnered Venezuela recognition as one of the world's best economies. In 1955, the *New York Times Magazine* described the Venezuelan economy as the most solid in the world.

Despite the military shake-ups at the top, it's hard to deny that in the mid-twentieth century, the social and economic stability was the best it had ever been. Contrary to popular beliefs, Venezuela's prosperity was not just based on its oil endowments. Actually, between the 1900s and 1960s, the country enjoyed high levels of economic freedoms. It had low regulations, low taxes, sound property rights, and a stable economic policy. In the 1950s, Venezuela was considered one of the world's wealthiest countries, with a GDP per capita of $7,424.00, which meant they were behind only three other nations; the United States, Switzerland, and New Zealand, respectively. I still hear stories from my grandparents, who grew their wealth during those golden years of Venezuela, and where many immigrants from the recently-ravaged Europe

kept pouring in. Yes, Venezuela kept encouraging European immigration. It was understood back then that the cultural values
were compatible with the growth Venezuela was experiencing.
My grandfather became an engineer in the capital city and became
an integral part of building the infrastructure of modern-day Venezuela. At the time, the country was experiencing such an economic bonanza that the middle class would often travel abroad
on the weekends for shopping, even finding that the value of the
dollar in the United States was cheaper than that of the bolivar. Of
course, that was brief. Venezuela, however, had become a place
where many wanted to move to, including many of the poorest
citizens of our neighboring countries. In the 70s and 80s, we experienced an unprecedented amount of immigration from Colombia. In Caracas, in the public maternity center, Concepcion Pala-
cios, there would often – even sometimes daily – be full foreign
mothers (Colombian, Ecuadorian, Peruvian), giving birth to their
children so they would be born with a Venezuelan citizenship.
Millions of poor Colombians crossed the border, and for humani-
tarian reasons, Venezuela took them in. Our public sector began
to collapse; it shouldn't surprise anyone that millions of poor Colombian migrants became a burden on the Venezuelan economy,
since, at the time, Venezuela's population did not even reach 20
million citizens. Who could have known, in a twist of fate, that
many of the descendants of those Colombians would eventually
cause the same kind of mass migration back to our southern
neighbor decades later?

However, let us take a step back to 1958, after the right-wing military leader, General Pérez Jiménez, was deposed from office and exiled. In 1958, Venezuela returned to a more "progressive" style of governance. A more "liberal" democracy, which General Pérez Jiménez had briefly corrected in terms of economic achievement. The new "liberal" government established a new constitution, which granted the state considerable powers over economic affairs. General Pérez Jiménez was considered an authoritarian by many, but in terms of the economy, he favored free markets, which allowed Venezuela to thrive under his rule.

Who was behind the return to "progressivism" in the Venezuelan government? None other than "Democratic" Rómulo Betancourt, whom many still see in history classes as one of "the good guys." He came back into office with his same communist ideals, but with the pretense that he was only left of center. To avoid past mistakes, he raised military salaries and gave its members all kinds of benefits; he even bought houses for many high-ranking officials. All the presidential decrees from his government seemed to be intended to destroy the country's productive industries. He would even appropriate land and give it to the workers of the land, rendering farming more inefficient than ever before. Betancourt was a machine when it came to signing decrees, and so ever-humorous Venezuelans would jokingly ask him for a decree prohibiting more decrees. Venezuela, under these progressive politicians, was in a downward spiral. Pérez Jiménez reappeared on the scene and campaigned for office once again. He was hugely popular because of his past leadership, which put the country on the map, despite what the propaganda might say. However, the government, sensing the threat posed by Pérez Jiménez, incapacitated him politically.

He wasn't "liberal" enough for the political elite at the time, however; so after he was overthrown, a pact was formed between Venezuela's two main political parties: "The Punto-Fijo Pact." The pact was a bipartisan agreement between "Acción Democrática" (Democratic Action, or AD), which was center-left, and COPEI (Christian Democrats), which was — supposedly — center-right. This pact meant that the two parties were to control the political arena from then on and take turns in governing the nation. Both parties, possibly well-intentioned (possibly), believed they could take petroleum revenues and channel them into welfare programs. They didn't believe that Venezuela could be fully independent and self-reliant unless the government had complete control of the oil revenues.

In the 1970s, those who wanted the nationalization of the oil industry, Venezuela's golden goose, got their wish. Early in the decade, then-President Carlos Andrés Pérez took advantage of the massive influx of petroleum rents — brought about by the 1970s energy crisis which occurred through the Western world — and took concrete steps to nationalize the oil industry. In 1975, President Pérez signed a law that finally nationalized the oil sector; therefore, the creation of the petro-state was complete. This completely transformed the Venezuelan economy and the foundation of society. Instead of relying on the citizens to pay their taxes in exchange for protecting their property rights and civil liberties, the Venezuelan government would now give handouts to its citizens by creating social programs and other public offerings that came from oil revenues. This gave the Venezuelan government more power than ever before as it was slowly training the citizens to become dependent upon it.

When Pérez was elected, he wasted no time spending lavishly when oil money started coming in and went on spending sprees while growing the social programs, but also increasing corruption within the government. Yes, this made Pérez and his party very popular with the masses because only a few realized the massive problems that were being created. The spending program coming from oil riches resulted in drifting further away from the decentralized idea that the nation's founders wanted; instead, the government became more and more centralized. Not to mention, the government fomented and encouraged a culture of fast spending which infected the population. This meant that the average Venezuelan became a fast spender and consumer of goods. Society was changing dramatically, and the gap between the rich and the poor just grew wider.

As we know, large governments hardly ever avoid the trap of corruption, so a staple of this style of petro-state governance was crony capitalism. What did that mean? That meant more lobbying and special interest groups. The state was becoming increasingly more concerned with the interests of corporate elites than with regular citizens. This, in turn, meant that those corporations also

spent more time lobbying the government for favors than producing the goods which the market demanded of them. Even though
the nationalization of oil did not create an immediate economic
collapse, it was the first thread of the already weak fabric to finally
break. The rest of the system would soon start to unravel. By the
start of the 1980s, the economy was growing stagnant. However,
because of Venezuela's privileged economic position in Latin
America, we started receiving migrants from neighboring countries, as I previously mentioned, mostly poor unskilled migrants
looking for economic opportunities. The GDP growth between the
60s and 90s grew at -0.13, meaning its population was growing
faster than its wealth. Soon after, our public services started being
overwhelmed, the population demographic began to change mas-
sively, and economic inequality between the rich and the poor increased.

With a stagnant economy and increased public debt caused by
the previous decade's spending binge, the Venezuelan government tried to take definitive action to jumpstart the economy. On
February 18th, 1983 — a day notoriously known in Venezuela as
Black Friday — the government implemented the largest devalu-
ation to its national currency to date. This marked the beginning
of a "lost decade" in Venezuela, where the GDP grew, but negatively. Now, let us remember Venezuela's "Punto Fijo Pact,"
where the two major parties essentially took turns to govern the
nation, even though elections were still freely held. By the late 80s,
it was AD, or Acción Democrática's turn, and the elected leader

of the party was Carlos Andrés Pérez, the man who had originally led the nationalization of the oil industry. Therefore, by 1989, Carlos Andrés Pérez became president of Venezuela for the second time; however, he came in with the promise and plan to revive the economy. Despite President Pérez's best intentions, perhaps it was too late at that point. The dependence from the poorest sectors had kept growing through the 80s and 90s, and social discontent was brewing throughout the nation because of the disparities between the classes. Carlos Andrés didn't follow the style of his first government and stayed away from heavy spending, which garnered him some enemies within his own party, and within the Venezuelan political elite, which was growing more accustomed to big government and stricter controls on the economy.

President Pérez then turned to the IMF for help with the economy. The recommendations included some sensible reforms, such as privatizing industries previously nationalized, plenty of government spending cuts, and tariff reductions. And he went to work on this; he privatized many industries such as CANTV (the largest telecommunications provider in the country), which started working much better. He implemented many of the IMF's recommendations. However, he would not touch PDVSA (the national oil industry or "Petróleos de Venezuela"). The reforms, however, seemed to be working, but there was plenty of political backlash even within his own party. Political tension was mounting. Because of the socio-economic divisions created between the 60s and 90s, some rogue ideologues in the military were ready to take him out. As mentioned, possibly the reforms to try to fix the country came a bit late. The Venezuelan population, especially the poor, had grown accustomed to high government spending and government dependence and therefore were not taking these reforms too positively.

In 1992, young lieutenant Hugo Chávez Frías led a military coup against President Carlos Andrés Pérez. He was an idealist, but his idealism led him and those who joined him in the coup to become murderers in the attempt to take out President Pérez and his family. Hundreds of people died on February 6th, 1992. At that point, Venezuela was the second longest-standing democracy in South America, after Colombia, and it was suffering a serious blow. However, loyal military forces were able to stop the attack, and the coup d'état against President Pérez failed. The rogue forces surrendered, many were killed in the attack from both sides, and Chávez conceded defeat on national television before he was taken prisoner. This military defeat was only a temporary victory for the government of Carlos Andrés Pérez; after that moment, there was definitely a collective sentiment that something had shifted.

The coup failed for a number of reasons; Chávez did not achieve his objective — which was to seize control of the media to call for a general uprising. Hundreds of people lost their lives, and after his rebel group had been subdued, Hugo Chávez surrendered to the media and seized this opportunity to talk to the public. He told his compatriots to surrender, noting that they would "fight another day" and that their surrender was only a temporary setback.

Some Venezuelan historians and politicians agree that this speech before the cameras before he went to prison was a turning point. A turning point where the general public fell in love with his words and Chávez gained his fame. Even wealthy patrons took notice of the fact that this man "had a way about him" and that he was a terrific speaker.

My grandfather on my father's side, whom his grandchildren nicknamed "Chacho," even recommended to my parents that they leave and start their family abroad, as neither my brothers nor I had been born yet. He believed democracy had fallen and that Venezuela would enter into a dark period. My family disagreed and preferred to stay in their homeland, feeling that my grandfather was being overly protective and paranoid. A year after the coup, Carlos Andrés Pérez was impeached from office on corruption charges and had to live in exile for the rest of his life. Only two years after Hugo Chávez went to prison, the government of President Calderas gave him a full political pardon, just another in a series of grave mistakes that were fundamentally chipping away at Venezuelan democracy. Chacho was right.

II

Marking the New Era
of Venezuela's Politics

I remember glimpses of the year 1998. It was an election year, and a carnival-like atmosphere prevailed throughout the country. At least it felt that way in the capital. I remember seeing banners for different political candidates of different parties: Irene Sáez, Henrique Salas Römer, Hugo Chávez Frías. There was a collective feeling that we were about to get a fresh start. Drawing closer to the December elections, my mom would pick me up from school. It was akin to a party in the streets, with different cars sporting the flags of their chosen candidate, people honking in support of each other, or jokingly shouting to someone that their candidate was better. It did not seem like a polarized nation back then, even though there were undoubtedly disagreements. I was only a child, and as I watched the situation, I simply asked my parents to explain. They told me they were supporting Henrique Salas Römer; others in the family supported Irene Sáez for the beautiful way she had transformed her district when she was mayor of Chacao. I had a couple of family members who believed in the "change" that Chávez offered. Irene Sáez had a lot of popular support initially until early in her campaign when she allowed herself to be associated with major political parties in the country. The same thing happened with Henrique Salas Römer, who initially campaigned independently, but eventually accepted the support of the traditional parties of the Punto Fijo Pact. The Venezuelan people were tired of the same elites, the same back and forth; therefore, many who had initially supported Salas Römer then threw their support to Chávez, as people saw him as someone who offered a unique way, a way out. Since the Punto Fijo Pact, politics had only allowed for two parties to rule for 40 years.

Obviously, many people had not forgotten what Chávez did in the 1992 coup d'état, which turned them against him and what they believed to be his empty promises. Despite that, however, Chávez had become the kind of political figure that seemed willing to take radical action to change the corrupt ways the country had fallen under. His message of 1992 to put down the weapons was still remembered as a positive thing by many when he said on national TV as the cameras clamored to him after the failed coup: "Friends, unfortunately, for now, the objectives we set for ourselves were not achieved in the capital city." Many remembered that "for now" as a promise of something better to come and saw Chávez as a military figure who was coming to help the nation change course. Unfortunately, that was not to be so, as Chávez only embodied the worst of the past governments. There was also the memory of Pérez Jiménez, who had signified economic progress in Venezuela like never before in the country. Since they both shared the trait of being military men, many citizens held the belief that it was men in the military who could cultivate a developmental government similar to Pérez Jiménez in the 50s, but with a less authoritarian style. Time has proven that that line of thinking was totally and completely wrong.

In his political campaign, however, Chávez presented himself as a level-headed candidate. Despite having visited Cuba shortly after his release from prison, he publicly stated that he rejected the Cuban government, its style of government, and communism. No doubt, guided at that moment by Fidel Castro himself, who knew that to have his man in the highest office in Venezuela, Venezuelans needed to consider him a moderate. Fidel Castro knew the technique well, as he denounced communism himself many times before he took Cuba and even gave a right-wing speech at the United Nations in New York. Castro knew how to sell his public image when he needed to, and he taught Chávez well. In October of 1996, Chávez toured the country and made public his plan for the nation. He published a document delineating such a plan. The text was "*A Democratic Revolution. Hugo Chávez's Proposal to Transform Venezuela*," where he indicated that the transition would be born out of what the country was going through in that period.

Before winning the election, Chávez had presented his plan for the Venezuelan economy, and it certainly sounded promising. As priorities, he established a plan to energize the Venezuelan economy; to establish a more humane economy that would be self-managed and competitive; to create a new relationship between society and the state, and to diversify industrial production. Chávez promised to end corruption, respect private industry, and allow for freedom of the press. The reality between his promises and his actions and results were quite different. His economy, in fact, had plenty of private industry appropriation by the government and nationalization of basic industries; such was the case for the endogenous paper industry (which resulted in a scarcity of toilet paper), the Lacteos Los Andes Dairy (resulting in a scarcity of pasteurized and powdered milk), the cement industry (resulting in a lack of cement), and some rice and sugar enterprises (leading to rice and sugar shortages). Obviously, his plan of re-energizing industries and creating more diversity of production was simply all talk.

Let's back up for a moment, as many might still be wondering how Hugo Chávez got out of prison in the first place. After all, this is what any reasonable person with any memory would ask. Hugo Rafael Chávez Frias was freed from prison for obscure reasons, but it had a lot to do with the enmity that President Rafael Calderas had for ex-President Carlos Andrés Pérez. Let me remind you here that Chávez attempted a coup against Pérez but failed. Eventually, the political elite managed to oust him from office on corruption charges a year after the coup. The president who followed Pérez was Caldera, another man who had been involved in Venezuelan politics for decades and who vehemently opposed the reforms Carlos Andrés Pérez attempted in his second government. Rafael Caldera was part of an elitist political group that saw the changing of the tides of the nation and believed that they needed to manufacture a leader that fit the nation's desires in order to keep control of the country behind the scenes. Historian Agustin Blanco Muñoz writes that while Chávez was in prison, President Caldera would send emissaries to him, allegedly to discuss his potential release and the conditions for it. As we know, Chávez was eventually pardoned and politically rehabilitated. Obviously, a huge mistake. The "manufactured" leader went rogue soon enough.

When he ran, Chávez was no longer the man in the green military uniform of '92, but a moderate in a suit and tie, shaking hands, promising to lift the poor out of poverty in two years, promising to end corruption and the four-decade rule of the Punto-Fijo Pact. That was music to the ears of many Venezuelans who were tired of stagnation. On December 6th, 1998, Hugo Rafael Chávez Frias won the presidential election, marking a new chapter in Venezuelan history. The celebration was monumental, as the country felt that, perhaps, there was a chance for renewal and revival towards the growth and safety the nation had experienced only a few decades earlier. Historian Blanco Muñoz said that, at the beginning of his first term, it seemed that the country was starting to walk along the path of real democracy, but that perception began to crumble quickly. Muñoz, who had many personal conversations with Chávez, describes him as a charming man and defines him as a master manipulator with a real talent for influencing and handling people. Muñoz said that for him, Chávez had defined himself as a caudillo early on in their conversations, where the president-to-be regularly defended other past Latin American caudillos.

In that 1998 election, he won the presidency with 56% of the vote. He told Venezuelans that their old model of oil dependence and corrupt politics was dead. He said that it was time to face reality. Chávez, as a new leader, was charismatic, and he was backed by many of the elite who believed they could control his economic agenda. He didn't look like the elites, however, so the poor were better able to relate to him as a leader, and he played up the fact that he had come from poverty straight into politics. Because apparently, no real business experience was a good thing. When he took office in 1999, the excitement of starting something new, something entirely different for the Venezuelan public, infected even those who voted against him. People were excited about this historical change, hoping something new and different was coming. We also thought it would be a new era of prosperity for Venezuela; we didn't think the new administration would destroy what had been achieved in the past. Polls show at the time that at least 90% of the country supported him and was rooting for him. It wasn't long, however, before that changed, and those who voted against him realized that they were right. Only three years later, there would be a movement to remove him from office, which accomplished its objective, but only for two days.

When Chávez won, United States ex-President Jimmy Carter said that a peaceful revolution had won and had begun in Venezuela. At the time, many viewed Chávez as the savior of the country. He certainly positioned himself as a second Simón Bolívar, coming to liberate the country from the so-called "Fourth Republic," which is how the period after Marcos Pérez Jiménez had been dubbed. He was not a savior, however; not anywhere close.

The Flood

A year after his historical win, heavy rains came to the northern part of the country. A storm caused flash floods resulting in debris flows, which lasted for days scattered across December, the same month Chávez was preparing to start a change to what he had called a "dying Constitution." The month of December was atypical for rain, so the storms took the country by surprise. The consequence was tens of thousands of deaths and destruction in what was called the "Vargas tragedy." Official figures say that around ten thousand died in the tragedy; however, extra-official statistics tell a different story, pointing to up to one hundred thousand, given that about eighty thousand body bags were ordered to collect the dead, and even those did not suffice. Furthermore, many people simply disappeared, and it is said they were swept out to sea.

The United States offered aid to the country, sending ships with relief. However, Chávez — allegedly advised by Fidel Castro — rejected the North American ships with the resolve of not starting his government tainted with the help of what he would, throughout his rule, deem the enemy of Venezuela. Many missionaries from Caracas and middle and upper-class families belonging to Christian schools pulled together and sent essentials to the affected area. However, Chávez's government would seize such necessities and brand them as if they had been sent by the government, crediting himself with the charity. Many people still believe that Chávez was the first politician in a long time who cared for the poor. Still, the reality was that he simply used them as a tool, as the poor have historically been used as a political instrument in Latin America and throughout the world. He exploited that tactic quite well by positioning himself as one of "the people" who also knew what it was like to be poor. What Chávez did was to use the political subject of "the poor" and use it in his favor, something still happening to this day with Nicolás Maduro. Unfortunately, this story is still believed by many of the humblest means in Venezuelan society, despite their dire circumstances.

What Hugo Chávez Frías did, in reality, was use the petro-state created in the 1970s for his own tyrannical and corrupt means, enriching himself and his inner circle. Chávez doubled down on the errors of the previous decades and brought the country to its knees through easy money, more economic controls, land confiscation, and vote-buying. The now-deceased president put his foot down on the accelerator of progressivism and doubled down on other interventionist projects that were laid out before he came into office. Chávez fed into the corruption he claimed to be against. One can clearly see this within own his family, which came from very humble beginnings to become one of the richest in the country, traveling in private planes across the world, and acquiring expensive residences in other nations. In just his first term, 6000 medium and small enterprises permanently shut down. Chávez also promised to fix the country and its rising rate of insecurity, but under him, it became exponentially worse. To deal with the problem of crime, he named his military ally, General Urdaneta, to lead the DISIP (General Sectoral Directorate of Intelligence and Prevention Services). After one year in office, Urdaneta went to Chávez to consult with him on his strategy to fight crime in Venezuela. Chávez responded that crime was not what he was interested in; what he envisioned for Venezuela was a political and ideological project.

The fact that Chavez wanted to turn the country into an ideological project seemed clear by his early actions, to anyone paying attention… or to those of us looking back. As early as October 2000, the Venezuelan President invited Fidel Castro to speak on his talk show "Aló Presidente" (Hello, President). It was a three hour show, and 57 minute show transmitted from the Carabobo field, where one of the most important battles of the Venezuelan War for Independence took place. Chavez and Castro spoke can-

didly about life, ideology, history, and where Chavez compli-
mented Fidel on the Cuban Revolution, a complete reversal from
what he had said earlier on the campaign trail.

His popularity in the voting booths on that 6th of December,
however, had been relegated to him alone, as when he won, his
party had not managed to win most other political seats. In fact,
Chávez's party did not win either house of Congress, any state
governments, the mayorships, or the communal boards; they all
remained in the hands of the opposition. Despite that, it seemed
that the opposition had fallen asleep, or they were permissive,
based on the president's early popularity, given that they allowed
Chávez to make a referendum to ask the people if they wanted to
change the Constitution. Why did the people allow this? Simply
because of the change he promised, the fresh start, and a departure from the old ways. They expected a change for the better that
might bring Venezuela into a new golden era. Therefore, Chávez
was allowed to start the process of changing the Carta Magna. To
do this, a Constituent Assembly was necessary, which was also to
be elected by the people. The Constituent Assembly was approved by a consultative referendum, which took place in April
1999. The country had just gone through an election, and only
37.65% of the electoral body participated. The opposition virtually
spent no effort to promote their candidates, and Chávez easily
won the majority of the seats in this temporary assembly tasked
with drafting a new constitution in six months. This temporary
Assembly was created to draft a new Constitution for Venezuela,

assuming absolute powers for those six months. This new Assembly eventually dissolved the Senate by converting the bicameral legislature, which consisted of a Congress with a Senate and a Chamber of Deputies, into a unicameral one, which only consisted of the National Assembly. They also created a new Constitution with a framework that better served Chávez's political project for the country.

However, the Assembly still had aspects of the old Constitution in place, which eventually ceased to matter as Chávez and his government routinely ignored the Constitution when governing on a whim and with people guarding the laws that were fundamentally allied to Chávez. The new Constitution, however, was a beginning since, in his first few years, Chávez had not fully cemented his power. Therefore, it allowed him to operate more freely. The new proposed Constitution recommended changing the presidential term from five to six years and changing the name of the nation from "República de Venezuela" (Republic of Venezuela) to "República Bolivariana de Venezuela" (Bolivarian Republic of Venezuela), presumably to reflect the second coming of Bolívar as the liberator of the nation. Of course, this second Bolívar was to be Chávez, according to him and his allies. This new Constitution was finally put to a vote in December of 1999, the same month when the country was experiencing a natural disaster. Chávez was advised to push back the voting process and prepare for the floods; however, he ignored this advice and continued with the referendum for the new Constitution, which he won again, thanks to his popularity and the lack of effort from the opposition. A few months later, Chávez called for new elections of all government bodies, including his own seat, for the purpose of "legitimizing his power," given the Constitutional changes. We all know now that this was simply political theater, but those "elections" re-legitimized him, renewed his term, and essentially re-started his presidency in 2000, for six years, ending in 2006.

In these elections, the opposition lost the National Assembly, leaving them with less than half the seats in the new one-chamber Congress and Chávez's political party with the majority of the seats, despite there being multiple opposition parties. This is what Venezuela had come to; a popularly voted, although never elected, subversion.

III

Don't Mess with My Children!

It was October of 2000 in Venezuela; Chávez had been president for less than two years when he dared touch something vital to the foundation of Venezuelan society: the family. He did this by going after education because he didn't consider children to belong to their parents but rather as assets of the state — assets that needed to be shaped and formed to fit his political ambitions.

At this time, I was still a kid; my concerns extended to who was inviting me to their birthday party, who wasn't, why my best friend was acting weird, and my homework. My parents picked me up from school every day, and every Friday, we would go to either of my grandparents' homes to hang out with any of my other 16 cousins (split between both sides of the family, of course). Most of us were blissfully unaware of what was happening to the nation, as we had little understanding of what was going on. Despite that, I remember often being dropped off by my parents at my grandmother's home, both of my parents dressed comfortably, ready to spend the whole of Saturday outside under the scorching sun, in political rallies and protests. When they got back, they would talk briefly about it, about Chávez, about his plans, and how the protests went. The seeds were being planted in my generation (albeit inadvertently) to become politically aware and politically active as we grew older.

That year, parents all across the nation, especially in my home city of Caracas, agreed to put a stop to Chávez's plans for radically changing education, both private and public. Parents and parent associations of different schools created a movement called "¡Con Mis Hijos No Te Metas!" (Don't Mess With My Kids!). The demand was directed at Hugo Chávez, who referred to the parents marching through the streets as "oligarchs," among other affronts. The movement was the first strong opposition effort against him and one that resulted in his retreat from his plans, at least for a time. Thousands upon thousands of people marched in the streets of Caracas to prevent the "Cubanization" of the education system. This became the primary theme of opposition to Chávez until 2001.

Chávez was forced to defend his position; he was forced to insist that he was not attempting to "Cubanize" Venezuela. However, he responded as if he wasn't affected; he responded by merely launching insults at his opponents. He responded by saying that the protests were small, that they were themselves evidence that the elites and the "oligarchy" of Venezuela were being defeated. He responded like a typical Latin American caudillo, which we were taught in school had been extinguished in Venezuela long before. Indeed, I remember being taught in school that the last "caudillo" had been General Marcos Pérez Jiménez (which, in hindsight, would have been preferable to Chavez a thousand times over).

So, what had happened? What exactly did Chávez do to garner such a response? Simple. That October, he put out a plan called "Decree 1011." He insisted the decree was his way of creating a "Bolivarian" education model that would guarantee the Venezuelan public an education that was free, public, compulsory, and of high quality.

Now many people of my generation in other nations hear "free" and jump for joy. Who doesn't love free, right? But a lesson that we all have to learn in this life is that nothing is free. Many people, media outlets, and non-governmental organizations knew to 'read between the lines' and actually read the decree, which Chávez insisted would go through, no matter what the opposition did or said. However, that didn't happen.

The Decree partially modified the teaching profession's regulations by creating new administrative figures, the "iterating" supervisors. These supervisors could be named directly by the Minister of Education and could influence both private and public education. It even allowed for these appointees to remove and assign school directors as they saw fit. Obviously, this ruffled some feathers as parents began to see apparent state interference with their children. Not to mention the most alarming aspect of the decree, which allowed Cuban teachers to be imported and be part of the arrangement.

The question was: why Cuban teachers? The salary for some of the social programs Chávez intended to implement was simply not enough for Venezuelan teachers. Therefore, Chávez made a deal with Cuba to hire people who would implement the Cuban style of education and Cuban supervision to execute the changes in exchange for cheaper oil.

The opposition vehemently opposed the Cuban interference. Of course, they also strongly disagreed with the so-called supervisors coming into the schools and "sticking their noses" into their curriculum. The private school association insisted that these supervisors would be a government mechanism to intervene in private education. The association threatened not to allow access to government officials to their institutions. Chávez responded to this by questioning what the private schools were hiding if he couldn't send in government officials to influence the schools. His tactic was to vilify the citizens who opposed him and pretend he supported the poor.

But the opposition to the education reform didn't extend just to private citizens; PROVEA (Venezuelan Human Rights Education and Action Program, a non-governmental organization focused on economic, social and cultural rights, expressed concern regarding various aspects of the program. The organization was apprehensive about the supervisors' limits. They considered that the conditions established to limit the supervisors' functions were not sufficient; the conditions contradicted the regulations already established under Venezuelan law and would most likely generate conflicts at other levels of education.

Critics believed this was an attack on the Venezuelan Constitution and Venezuelan freedoms. Some even went so far as to say that because families felt their children were targets of this government intervention, it was a tactic by Chávez to later go after private property with more permissiveness from the general society because it wasn't quite as controversial as directly going after the family.

That might well be true, but it doesn't take away from the fact that Chávez tried to push through an educational reform again in 2008. After he died, the government he left behind has attempted the same thing with slight modifications over and over again. In fact, his 2007 attempt was the primary reason I left Venezuela to pursue an education elsewhere.

In reality, it all points to the fact that Chávez merely sought to use the school system as an ideological weapon to indoctrinate future generations of students to fit his political agenda — a political project that would orient the nation to a socialist, progressive leftist model. The way to do this was through political control of the teachers. A blatant attempt was made in the "Decree 1011," then through the ideologization of students, the effort to create a biased curriculum, and budget restrictions to attempt to break the autonomous university, and the famous "Missions."

Anyone has to be willfully blind to ignore the attempt by Chávez to shape the minds of future Venezuelans, but what some disagree on is what Chávez wanted the results to be. To his opposition, Chávez wished to have future generations of Venezuelan students grow up with the goal of maintaining and perpetuating his "revolution" and socialism in Venezuela. Someone that was more charitable to Chávez might hope that he was simply trying to level the playing field, trying to serve the most disadvantaged members of society by giving them the quality of education only middle-class students and upper-class students seemed to be receiving in private institutions.

The reality, though, was quite different; his policies led public education, whose students are some of the poorest in society, to increasingly higher levels of academic precariousness. The obvious conclusion is that the Chavista "revolution" created an inferior education for the poor. Instead of making the education market more competitive, he made it more difficult for private institutions to survive and maintain their quality. It seemed that his attempt was to lower education quality across the board instead of raising the quality of the public system.

His political project of control never saw education as a path to train students to become professionals in their fields with critical thinking skills; his intention was not to advance and promote scientific and technological development in Venezuela. No. His aim was to have followers who would reinforce his ideas and his "socialism of the 21st Century" for decades to come.

It was apparent to many, and now to many more looking back, that he was attempting to create what the Italian Marxist philosopher, Antonio Gramsci, had coined as "Cultural Hegemony." The kind of cultural conformity that was needed to peacefully maintain socialism. The idea was, and still is, to create a society that conforms and internalizes socialist values to have a population that unites under the government's ideology. An ideology that moved far away from the spirit of what Venezuela used to be; a country that had long emulated the spirit of freedom in Latin America since the war of independence.

Earlier, I mentioned the "Missions" or "Misiones," and I think it's important to talk about them given that many leftists worldwide will point to this cornerstone of Chávez's education plan. They will marvel at how the "revolution" reached places most Latin American governments could only dream of. They will talk about his love for the people, making the "Missions" an example of that love. The reality was, those "Missions" were only a façade.

By now, maybe you are wondering, what are the "Missions"?

In 2003, Chávez formed assistance programs that he labeled "Missions." They were created coincidentally after a considerable effort by the opposition, which collected signatures calling for a referendum to remove Hugo Chávez from the presidency. Regardless of how young I was, I remember my parents being part of the effort, just like thousands of other Venezuelans. I remember that we managed to get the signatures and were getting ready to call for a referendum, as the constitution allowed. However, Chá-vez's government put up all kinds of obstacles, delays, and efforts to create a surge in popularity among their base: in came the social programs, the "Missions."

The referendum was delayed, but the Missions were put in place to attend to the immediate needs of the poor. The intent was to create a sense that the government cared for them selflessly, thereby creating a sort of "quick" support for his regime based on instant gratification.

One of the Missions was called "Mision Barrio Adentro." Mision Barrio Adentro loosely translates to "Inner-City Mission" and consisted of installing primary health care modules in the most impoverished neighborhoods in Caracas and in marginal areas which surrounded important cities throughout the country. This sounds great, in theory, however, here we are inching our way toward a dependent population. There was also a lack of imme-diately available Venezuelan medical personnel willing to work for the pay that was offered. So this led Chávez to establish an agreement with none other than Fidel Castro and the Cuban gov-ernment. Again, Cuban doctors for more oil. There was a point during Chávez's presidency that Venezuela practically became the lifeline of Cuba and its dictatorship. That quick setup garnered him easy sympathy from the voters of those impoverished sectors, and, as mentioned, made them dependent.

But this is about education and the Chavista regime's interfer-ence in education, so let's stay on that subject. The other Mission was the "Mision Robinson." This one was about education, specifically, about educating the poor with alternative education. Its goal was to teach the population who hadn't had a chance to obtain formal schooling. Mision Robinson practiced the same arrangement with Cuba as Mision Barrio Adentro, teachers and teaching supplies from Cuba in exchange for oil.

Both missions accomplished what they set out to do: to propel the collective consciousness. To convince people that Chávez wanted the collective good, seeking nothing in return. In the educational mission, the same methods used as propaganda in Cuba for indoctrination in 1961 were used on Venezuela's poorest and most vulnerable. Thanks, Fidel. A massive propaganda campaign was launched all across the country, where people would come on-screen with their testimonies about learning to read, thanks to Chávez's revolution. Foreign governments extended their congratulations; the Venezuelan Government even put out a statement bragging that UNESCO had declared Venezuela a land free of illiteracy and that Venezuela had become an example to the world. However, it wasn't long until that statement was recalled, as many people called it into question and found it was false. In 2006, Aristóbulo Istúriz, the Minister of Education, had to publicly admit that the declaration of a "land free of illiteracy" had not come from the international organization but was instead a sovereign declaration of the Venezuelan government.

Was their declaration in any way close to the truth, though? Was the Venezuelan government making huge strides in eradicating illiteracy? Of course, they would say yes, their propaganda hinged on that assertion... but not quite. The truth is that UNESCO considers illiteracy in a country to have been defeated when the rate is lower than 4%. In 2001, the illiteracy rate in Venezuela was around 6%. Ten years later, after over ten years of the Chavista government, and after hundreds of thousands of public funds had been spent for social programs and propaganda, the improvement was marginal. As a country, we went down to a 5% illiteracy rate, but our ties to the Cuban government were stronger than ever, not to mention the poor's dependency on Chávez as a savior figure.

The educational and scholastic mission that they so boasted about was not achieved. Given that Venezuela's illiteracy rate had been falling at a steady rate before Chávez was elected, it's hard to say that the 1% difference in ten years was attributed to his missions. However, the real goal of the missions was undoubtedly achieved. The electoral mission, the whole Chavista team, did achieve its electoral objective. It gave fish to the poor, but it did not teach them to fish. The poor now believed they were dependent on Chávez and that he was their protector.

Nowadays, unsurprisingly, Mision Robinson, as it was famously named, is practically nonexistent. Obviously not because they eradicated illiteracy, even though that is the government's claim. Its real objective had been fulfilled. It was no longer needed for votes. And were the students of the missions successful? Not quite. Many of them couldn't compete with students who emerged from formal education systems and (here I am talking about the students from the "Misiones") weren't admitted to universities because they lacked the skills they needed.

Chávez's government also created parallel schooling, with fewer school subjects and fewer requirements. This was supposedly to level the playing field, to integrate more students who weren't able to get an education in the school system. All it did was to give students a high-school diploma that, in the end, was worth nothing. The parallel school system was not producing capable professionals but people with high-school diplomas that the government would recognize. Instant gratification. If they could not get further in life, it was due to some sort of systemic oppression that was present to only benefit the so-called "oligarchs," or so Chávez claimed.

Schooling and education under the Chavista government have had it as a mission to ensure that the generations coming up in Venezuelan society today have cohesion around the support for a politically partisan project that aims to replace the democracy that was re-established in Venezuela in 1958. Chávez used education as an ideological weapon. He never expected education to serve the purpose of individual development and social progress.

As mentioned earlier, the year 2007 was the second time Chávez and his government tried to push for educational reform within the standard school system; so far, it had only been implemented in parallel schooling and the missions. This time I was in high school; this time, I made the decision to leave. Why? I believed my education, along with my future, was being called into question. I was not the first among my peers to leave, but I certainly was not the last. Many of my friends are now scattered across the world, many of my family members as well. At the time, of course, it almost felt like a pre-emptive measure, but one that I never regretted. Although I have always felt a sense of melancholy about what it would have been like to study along with my friends in universities in Caracas that I respected, such as "Simón Bolívar University," nicknamed "la Simón," or "The Metropolitan University," nicknamed "la Metro," or where my mom had gone "La Católica," The Catholic University in Caracas. But that was not to be.

In 2007, they went after the formal school system again, with a curriculum plan to create a "Bolivarian School System." Its content was so blatantly propagandistic and ideological that it was denounced by teachers' unions, universities, educational unions, the National Academies, and non-governmental organizations, such as the Education Assembly and the National Federation of Parents. Ideologization by the government was not a mere accusation by the vast opposition; it was an admission by Chávez's government itself. They had openly stated its intention to indoctrinate students; proof of that was an assertion by Aristóbulo

Istúriz, former education Minister and most recently vice-president, who in 2006 blatantly said to the media, "In education, we are ideologizing, so what?"

The pressure from institutions, however, was so pronounced that Chávez was forced to stop his plan and shelve it; but we all knew that was just a momentary strategy. The proposed curricular design established that its objective was to form a new kind of citizen related to the new model of society that the political machine wanted to be implemented in the country. To provide some examples of the change in curriculum, we can go to the teaching of history. In Venezuelan history as a subject, some omissions were called into question, such as skipping over the Rule of Marcos Pérez Jiménez, perhaps because of the social and economic growth Venezuela experienced through his time, despite the authoritarianism. The curriculum also barely covered the period between 1958 and 1999. It mostly recounted problems during that period and highlighted the idea that the Venezuelan elites were to blame for the hardships. "The rich" being the problem was a Chavista talking point since day one, and now they planned to teach it in schools. The proposed school curriculum for history also apologized for any governmental acts during Chávez's time, which amounted to propaganda. Furthermore, the proposed curriculum also made military topics a priority above other subjects in the last two years of high school.

Yes, Chávez shelved the plan, but the curriculum proposal came back again after his death in 2013, slightly modified, but still highly politicized, full of propaganda and ideology. The curriculum this time had an outline that directly went against the Venezuelan Constitution, which stated in Article 102 that education was for "developing the creative potential of each human being and the full exercise of their personality in a democratic society." Instead, what we were getting with the so-called "Plan Patria" for education was the objective to preserve "Bolivarian liberating values of equality and solidarity of the Venezuelan people, and to promote the development of a new socialist ethic." What on earth? Anyone with the ability to comprehend can see the issue here. One of the objectives of this new plan was to have the education sector "adapt the study plans at all levels to include strategies for the formation of socialist and patriotic values."

Chávez had distributed hundreds of thousands of school textbooks to the public schools. In the history books, unsurprisingly, about 50% of the stories were about him. In a country with a 200-year history since Independence and roughly half a millennium after its discovery, it made no sense that 50% of the story was dedicated to a man who had only been president for less than 2% of that time. Textbooks also glorified the youth of the 1960s, who tried to generate in Venezuela something similar to the Cuban revolution. The textbooks ignored Cuba sending guerilla forces to Venezuela; they also glorified the attempted coup d'état in 1992 by Chávez, framing the incident as a heroic democratic act.

Education was really going down the drain by other means, even if the Chavista government was not having an easy time directly implementing their curriculum changes. By the end of 2014, more than 1,600,000 people had left the country, the majority of them university professionals. The brain drain was and is massive. By July 2017, a university professor in Venezuela with 16 years of service, a doctorate, published work, and with the highest achievement in a teaching career received a salary equivalent to $50 a month at the exchange rate on the black market — equivalent to $97 on the official exchange controlled by the government to which only a few privileged sectors and those friendly with the government have access. Who wouldn't leave if they had the chance? By 2017, more than 1,400 professors had resigned from the two most prestigious universities in the country, the Central University of Venezuela and the Simón Bolívar University. The number increases every year, although obtaining official numbers in Venezuela becomes more challenging every day.

Yes, in the early 2000s, there *was* an increase in school enrolment because of government programs, but we know the real objective of this and the results those programs had. The goal was never to raise the quality so that the poor would have equal or greater education and access to private schools. Schooling by Chávez and his "progressive" government has failed in Venezuela, which shouldn't surprise anyone. The Education Minister once famously said: "Don't believe that we are going to educate everyone so that later they improve their social position and become '*escu-alidos.*'*" Good education is an obstacle for authoritarianism and socialist governments, so they make education itself an obstacle to free thought.

---

* *Escualido*, was the expression with which Chavez stigmatized anyone who disagreed with his political projects, usually people of middle and upper class backgrounds.

IV

The "Cubanization" of Venezuela

When I was in the 5th grade, I remember sitting in recess with my friends, and while eating our mid-morning snacks, we would be discussing what we were hearing from our parents and families. In our less eloquent 5th grader language, we were speculating about the political situation Venezuela found itself in. One of us remarked that Venezuela was practically responsible for freeing half of the Latin American continent; 'we know what freedom is and that Cubans didn't understand it quite as clearly' we would quip. Another one of us would tell stories of Cubans informing on their neighbors who were political opponents of Castro and how that could never happen here. We would be amazed that anyone would report or make lists of people they disagreed with. I remember our conversations during recess, a group of 11-year-old girls trying to convince ourselves that nothing that happened in Cuba could ever happen to us. For me, preteens knowing about such things was normal because it was part of conversations in our families, talks amongst adults at cocktail parties, and even birthday parties. I often listened to political talk shows on the radio during my morning ride to school in my mom's car, and so did my friends. But we were certainly naïve.

The relationship between Venezuela and Cuba has radically changed over the years. It has been far from traditional, especially these last few years. The two countries' history shows that their relationship has gone from cordial to non-existent to friendly, until eventually the lines distinguishing each individual country became a blur. Is the relationship between Venezuela and Cuba strange? Can we say that maybe the relationship between these two nations is no longer definable by the word "foreign"? From what we understand foreign to be, then perhaps it's hard to make the case that the two countries have a normal relationship for two foreign nations. Foreign literally means "strange, outer, external…" In medieval Latin, the word *"foraneus"* means "on the outside of doors." The reason to be specific is to make sure we know what is being talked about. There is no question, then, that a foreign nation should be a completely and utterly external factor when it comes to the domestic affairs of a country.

Nations that deal internally with another and create agreements that directly and openly affect their internal policies are unswervingly challenging their "foreign" relationship; thereby, their affiliation ceases to be a matter of foreign policy but rather of domestic policy. This is not to mean trade agreements or cultural exchanges; this means when citizens' national barriers and nationalities become interchangeable. The two countries then seem to be taking the political shape of one, even if not represented by a geographical map. In the case of Venezuela and Cuba, this was done slowly, without the consent of the general population, and against their own constitutional laws. At the moment, and for some time now, Cuba makes major Venezuelan decisions, including administrative, economic, and military decisions. Venezuela, on the other hand, makes no decisions for Cuba but rather constantly consults with the Cuban government on how to deal with the internal policies that Cuba does not already control.

This is why I believe these two nations have an "unconventional" relationship (to say the least). They are two countries that seem to be merging, so Venezuelans colloquially give it the name of "Cubazuela" because many of us don't believe it is solely Venezuela anymore. The name actually came from the late Venezuelan President Hugo Chávez Frías; he seemed to take some kind of pride in the excessive union. However, the union is not a two-way street. It's an unequal alliance where Cuba has the upper hand. It is as if, for example, a small country, were to control the United States. This is why to really understand the "amalgamation" of the two, it's essential to look back and try to understand how Cuba and Venezuela have made it to this interesting point in their history.

Past events are never isolated. They are never part of a single story but can influence the course of other nations and of people who were not necessarily involved in the first place. These two Latin American nations established a diplomatic relationship shortly after Cuba gained its independence from Spanish rule in 1902. Until the 1950s, the two countries had maintained a cordial but standard relationship that was not significantly different from others in the region. So, what happened in the 1950s? Plenty happened.

As I have mentioned in a previous chapter, in 1952, General Marcos Pérez Jiménez took power in Venezuela; he did this by halting an election and declaring himself president using his military muscle. His government was exceptionally right-wing — especially when it came to economics. Even though there was a lack of a democratic process, the country did nothing but improve financially and in terms of infrastructure during Jiménez's rule. When he was unseated in 1958, after six years in office, a provisional government replaced Jiménez until elections could be held, and a new president take office. The provisional government was comprised of naval officer Wolfgang Larrazábal and lawyer Edgar Sanabria. Finally, when the elections came around, the country got a new president: Rómulo Betancourt.

At this point, you may be wondering: why is this relevant? Well, around the same time that Venezuela was going through this transition, Cuba also saw a dictator take power in 1952 — coincidentally at the same time as General Pérez Jiménez. Cuba's new ruler was Fulgencio Batista, a military man and political leader who had ruled Cuba even before his dictatorship. Batista had had a successful government the first time around, and when he returned to power in 1952, he did it by first deposing the previous president in a bloodless coup d'état which was mostly welcomed by the Cuban population, given the widely unpopular and unsuccessful presidency of Carlos Prío. Batista's second government, however, had every aspect of a dictatorship. He controlled the National University, the press, the Congress, and he embezzled huge amounts of funds. He also jailed political opponents and used terrorist methods to impose his rule. It was at the end of 1958 when the opposition within his country started a revolution. The socialist leader Fidel Castro, who defeated Batista's forces and took power early in 1959, led this revolution.

It's funny how history sometimes gives us these interesting coincidences. Notice how the dates almost coincide with Venezuela's coup d'état. General Marcos Pérez Jiménez took power in 1952, just like Fulgencio Batista. Then the Cuban Revolution against Batista was only a year after Venezuela was able to topple Pérez Jiménez. The Venezuelan democratic leaders related to Cuba's struggle in 1958, and there was almost a moral need to help them or to support their left-leaning comrades. Yes, there were meetings in Caracas by Cuban opposition groups that were doing everything they could to get rid of Batista. Their plan, however, was to elect Manuel Urrutia to the government, which they did, but he lasted only a few months. However, the Venezuelan capital happened to be just one of the places where many groups met to raise funds for those in Cuba who were planning the revolution; the other cities were Miami and Mexico City. Some say that Wolfgang Larrazábal sent weapons to Sierra Maestra, where the Cuban revolutionaries were plotting their insurrection. Whether that is true or not, we know the Venezuelan leader was aware of their plans and gave Cuban opposition leaders the green light to meet in Caracas. Perhaps, the Venezuelan naval officer believed Cuba was trying to achieve what Venezuela had recently accomplished; a peaceful transition of power from an authoritarian leader to a democracy. Who could predict that communism would take over Cuba for the next 60 years and counting?

We all know what happened. In 1959, Fidel Castro consolidated his presidency with no intention of holding democratic elections. He was to continue his revolution and impose his socialist/communist vision on his country. His first trip abroad after this consolidation of power was to none other than Venezuela in 1959, where he was welcomed as yet another Latin American leader who managed to free his people from dictatorial oppression. Now, in hindsight, how ironic. One of the purposes of Castro's trip was to discuss the financing of his revolution. Remember Rómulo Betancourt? The Venezuelan president who was elected in place of Wolfgang Larrazábal?

President Betancourt met with Castro. At that time, Betancourt already doubted the democratic intentions of the bearded "progressive" leader. Although Betancourt was a "quasi-communist" and very left-leaning, he saw himself as a democratic leader and was a far cry from the radical that was Fidel. When they both met in private, the Cuban revolutionary asked President Betancourt for Venezuelan funds to back his revolution. His argument was that the two countries were "one" in the pursuit of freedom for the Latin American people and that they should join together and help each other. His request amounted to 300 million dollars and subsidized oil prices, or if the Venezuelans could spare it, free oil. His request didn't go over too well. Although Betancourt was not a right-wing leader but somewhat left-leaning, he still respected democracy, or at least the appearance of democracy. He didn't believe Castro represented that. So, to Castro's dismay, Betancourt refused the request. It didn't take long until the relationship between the two countries started to seriously suffer and, in 1961, Venezuela broke off diplomatic relations with the island on the grounds of finding it undemocratic and an enemy to Venezuela's core values. How things have changed... At the time, of course, that did not sit well with Castro.

It is interesting to point out that while all this was happening, external forces came into play that influenced Castro's moves and decisions. In 1959, the Cuban revolutionary flew to New York City at the invitation of the American Society of Newspaper Editors. At the time, the Eisenhower administration was in place, and the president of the United States had strong reasons to believe that Castro and his companions (his brother and Che Guevara) were communist sympathizers. Now, it is easy to look back and think it was obvious that Castro was a communist; however, back then,

Castro merely labeled himself a "progressive" and a revolutionary seeking the liberation of his nation. President Eisenhower disliked Castro's views on the Cold War and his opinion of Nasser in Egypt. Castro had a positive view of the Soviet Union, and he shared the "anti-imperialist" view of Nasser. It was rumored that Castro wanted to meet with Eisenhower, but the U.S. president snubbed the Cuban leader.

It was not long, however, until Russia started paying attention to the Caribbean island. In February 1960, the USSR sent representative Anastas Mikoyan to Cuba to evaluate whether Castro was working for American interests or if he really was a communist leader. Mikoyan was sent under the pretext of inaugurating a Soviet trade division. It was during this visit that a five-year trade agreement was signed between the USSR and Cuba. The Soviet country promised to buy one million tons of sugar annually, giving petroleum products in exchange. Since Cuba had been denied Venezuela's oil, this seemed like a good deal.

It may seem as if this partnership would be the end of Cuba's courtship to obtain Venezuelan money, but that was not the case. Ernesto "Che" Guevara had an opinion about Soviet "intrusion" in Cuban affairs. He was uncomfortable that the Caribbean nation had to depend on the northern empire, so he again suggested that Venezuela would be the perfect place to spearhead Cuba's revolution into the rest of the Latin American countries; so Fidel Castro again started devising a plan to obtain patronage from the prosperous oil nation — and with Venezuela having cut off its relationship to Cuba — Castro decided that this time he wouldn't ask, but would try to get it by force.

In the early 1960s, while Venezuela was under Betancourt's leadership, Castro was secretly starting his incursion into Venezuela after the South American government had helped Cubans escape their country following their part in the failed Bay of Pigs invasion. The relationship between the two Caribbean nations further deteriorated. Castro had sent people into Venezuela to recruit people into his communist guerrilla army. Dozens of police officers, national guards, and civilians, including women and children, were killed in Castro's search for people who would join him and his socialist agenda for Venezuela. The discovery of these plans in 1963 caused Rómulo Betancourt to go to the Organization of the American States (OAS) and provide evidence that Cuba was storing weaponry on Venezuela's shores. This was enough for the OAS to expel Cuba from the organization and for all member countries (except Mexico), to terminate diplomatic ties with the island.

In 1967, Venezuela suffered an incident, barely remembered in history, but essential to better understand the Cuba-Venezuela relationship. This episode is what is known as the "Machurucuto Incident." In this particular event, twelve Cuban-trained guerillas, a majority of whom were Cuban-born, except for a few Venezuelans trained in Cuba, came into Venezuela by sea, intending to gather more Venezuelan guerrilla forces. This was a strategy to topple the democratically-elected president, Raúl Leoni. However, the so-called "incident" did not go as planned: the Venezuelan army and the National Guard engaged them and killed ten of them while also taking two prisoners, both Venezuelan born, and who are now, ironically, part of the Chavista government and entourage.

One of the Venezuelan guerrilla members involved with Castro for years is now an author who wrote about the tumultuous relationship that existed between the two nations and about the relationship today. His name is Hector Pérez Marcano, a front-row witness to Castro's plans for Venezuela and a member of the National Liberation Front in the 1960s. He recounts how important Castro believed it was for Venezuela to help Cuba, or rather for Cuba to help themselves by using Venezuela. It all goes back to one thing: Venezuela's oil. Many Americans will point to the idea that oil would be a reason for the U.S. to go after Venezuela, not Cuba. However, diplomatic ties between the U.S. and Venezuela had been strong for 100 years. Politically, it made no sense for the U.S. to invade their ally. It was the United States, after all, who helped Venezuela set up its oil fields. Marcano, the ex-guerrilla soldier, affirms that Castro had firmly set his sights on the South American country's oil as soon as he came to power; and even though his plans for getting it had to change along the way, the certainty that he needed Venezuelan oil never floundered.

So, is Venezuela's "Black Gold" a blessing or a curse?

Everything that has led to the debacle Venezuela now faces seems to have one single factor in common — and that is its oil reserves. Oil should not be a negative factor for a country's stability or progress, but an advantage, especially with the world's demands. The black gold, however, as many like to call it, is simultaneously Venezuela's blessing and curse. Especially since the nationalization of the oil industry. The revenue from the oil exports falling into the wrong hands could mean the facilitation of considerable corruption — and that seems to be what is happening today.

Why does Venezuelan oil attract so much attention? The answer is probably simply because this small South American country has the most extensive oil reserves in the world, with over 300 billion barrels. The fact that Venezuela has so much oil isn't so relevant when it can't even secure enough investment to unlock the resource or when it destroys its oil fields... However, it becomes quite interesting when we pay attention to China's involvement in the country. Getting to control those oil fields means unlocking an oil network of about 30 trillion dollars. That is enough to pay the collective national defense budget of every single nation in the world combined, multiple times. So, while many people will pay no mind to the political reasons behind the informal "Cubazuela" and other foreign interests, they should just look at the numbers and the money that this country could potentially control. Venezuela has massive amounts of oil, and it also possesses the second-largest natural gas resource in the Americas. Inversely, however, it is one of the worst-performing economies in the hemisphere.

Would anyone ever wonder if Cuba interfering in Venezuelan affairs is perhaps a good idea? That Venezuelans questioning that are just being conspiratorial? Maybe Cuba's need for oil is merely humanitarian, and Venezuela is just being a good neighbor. The Castro brothers could have arguably been the most powerful and sinister minds of the hemisphere in the past century. Is that a stretch? Imagine if those brothers had been at the helm of a more powerful nation. They have managed to have their country stuck in the 1950s for 60 years. These two men are not only sinister but very smart. These accusations are not hollow, but they can be backed by facts, even if the allegations are abstract in nature.

The Castro brothers have survived hundreds of assassination attempts, many of them by the CIA. The late Fidel Castro once joked that if surviving assassination attempts were an Olympic sport, he should win a medal. Their dictatorship outlasted that of the Soviets, even with their dwindling economy. As mentioned, they have managed to keep their population stuck in time. That is a difficult feat in the twenty-first century world that we live in. Granted, since Raul Castro, and later Miguel Díaz-Canel, have been ruling over the island, things have not been as strict as when Fidel Castro was presiding over it with an iron fist. However, this poor Caribbean island has managed to become incredibly influential, with more than nine armed nations following its footsteps by pledging loyalty to the island. It is estimated that Venezuela gave between 6 to 8 billion dollars a year to Cuba, up until 2020. This amount of "aid" is almost two times greater than what the Soviet Union provided for the island during the Cold War.

To put it in perspective, Cuba's economy fell by 35% in 1991 after the USSR collapsed. Therefore, without Venezuela's aid, Cuba's influence would shrink, and so would its economy. Possibly the Castrista regime now carried on by Miguel Díaz-Canal, would collapse unless the rumors are true that other eastern nations are stepping in to fill that gap. But that's a conversation for another day. Venezuela and Cuba trade their oil in exchange for political allegiance and loyalty. They trade for other countries' silence in the face of their shady dealings. They trade it for an image. These countries that align together with Venezuela and Cuba have something more in common than corruption in the face of oil money. They believe in an ideology — at least that is what they started with and what they keep feeding their populations through propaganda and "free" education. What holds them together is a common enemy: a hatred for the United States. This is not exactly a secret.

Venezuela's late President Hugo Chávez has made it public on numerous occasions that the United States is "evil." Most famously, when he said that Bush smelled like sulfur in a UN conference, to imply that Bush must have come from Hell. Iran, China, and North Korea are just a couple of examples of nations that have formed a friendship with these two Latin American countries in the past 20 years. To the concern of the United States, Venezuela has also given considerable quantities of uranium to Iran for its nuclear program. Groups like Hezbollah have been aided and hidden by the Venezuelan government. FARC gets support, shelter, and weapons from the Chavista regime. Essentially, Venezuela has become the largest cartel in the world and a state-sponsor of terrorism.

How is it that Venezuela has been able to get away with such a massive con? Oil money is the most basic answer. The Venezuelan government knows that it must keep up democratic appearances so that the rest of the world does not meddle or call the Venezuelan government "a dictatorship" or a "terrorist nation." These tactics have somehow worked, although lately it seems that the world is starting to wake up to the false democracy that Venezuela has become. The fact that the international public does not seem to pay much attention to what goes on in Venezuela, or Cuba, however, has given a lot of room for these governments to maneuver.

The Venezuelan government, starting with Chávez, has invested millions of dollars in campaigns and the electoral process, which, except for ex-U.S. Democrat President Jimmy Carter, countless international experts have condemned as fraudulent. Doesn't North Korea hold elections? Doesn't Cuba? Yes. They do. All Venezuela needed, however, was an outside organization that vouched for the transparency of their elections. I mentioned Jimmy Carter, so here is where the Carter Center comes in. The

Carter Center has provided Venezuela with the leverage they have needed on the international stage. Jimmy Carter even called Venezuela's election process "the best in the world." That is very questionable, considering that in plain sight anyone can see armed groups roaming through the streets on Election Day, screaming government slogans and threatening the opposition. The Carter Center is sustained by several Middle East regimes, which "coincidentally" share deep political ties with the Venezuelan government. Even the family of the late terrorist Osama Bin Laden donated over a million dollars to the Carter Center. Does that raise any red flags yet?

The Era of Hugo Chávez aka "El Comandante"

Let's take it back a bit until it really came together for Fidel Castro. Remember his wish? His stubborn desire for influence over Venezuela? Fidel Castro had on multiple occasions tried and failed to violently gain influence over the South American nation. His relationship with Venezuela has remained unfriendly for years until finally, President Rafael Caldera forgave Cuba for its transgressions. There is no solid evidence to suggest that Castro was planning a more diplomatic and/or deceitful way to obtain the oil. Still, it could be argued that he was just waiting for the right Venezuelan to make his move. In 1992, after the failed but notorious coup by Hugo Rafael Chávez, Castro set his sights on Chávez.

After President Calderas set things in motion by pardoning Chávez and rehabilitating him politically, the Cuban leader invited him to the island. A young hopeful Chávez is welcomed in Cuba as if he was a foreign leader. It was a two-day visit. Allegedly, Fidel and Hugo would stay up for hours discussing politics and the Marxist ideology. Chávez described that encounter many times with nostalgia. "Fidel saw that Chávez was a diamond in the rough, and he started to polish him," former Venezuelan officials remarked. Analysts agree that Mr. Castro saw Chávez as a politically naïve mark.

Even though the coup in 1992 had failed, it gave Chávez and his companions some time to reflect on their failure and plan for their future success. In prison, they realized that the most effective way to create change and not alienate the Venezuelan public, which still had democratic values ingrained, would be to start a political project. The movement, which had started as a revolutionary military undertaking, became a political party by the name of "Movimiento Quinta República" (MVR), meaning "Movement of the Fifth Republic." It was clear the intention was to fundamentally change Venezuela. Chávez was the head of MVR, and as such, began making alliances with smaller left-leaning political parties. This new party became a "true opposition," compared to the old party system, which only had a few minor policy differences.

After Chávez was elected for the first time, he traveled to Havana only days before he was sworn in as president. Again, he goes to Cuba! On this trip, he also met the Nobel laureate, Gabriel García Márquez. The writer was only a newspaper writer back then, and he had been commissioned to write a profile of Hugo Chávez. After meeting him, he wrote on the profile that Chávez "had an immediate friendliness and a homegrown charm that was unmistakably Venezuelan." The profile continued narrating Chávez's story, revealing the newly-elected president's indignation with the social inequality in Venezuela. García Márquez ended the profile with what could perhaps be a prediction: "While he sauntered off with his bodyguards of decorated officers and close friends, I was overwhelmed by the feeling that I had just been traveling and chatting pleasantly with two opposing men. One to whom the caprices of fate had given an opportunity to save his country. The other, an illusionist, who could pass into the history books as just another despot."

Only a year after this encounter in Havana, Chávez invited Castro to his hometown: Sabaneta, Venezuela. Chávez strolled through memory lane with his new mentor, and right then and there, in the year 2000, the first oil deal was signed between the two nations. What Castro had wanted since the late 1950s with multiple Venezuelan presidents, he got within the first year of the Chávez presidency... and more was still to come. The deal provided Cuba with 3,000 barrels of oil per day while Cuba gave Venezuela political advisors. Did we really need political advisors from this communist dictatorial nation? Chávez seemed to think so. Imagine the U.S. importing political advisors from a foreign nation because this was almost the equivalent of that. It was a good time for Cuba to be receiving these oil royalties, given that, historically, the price of this commodity was about to get higher than ever before as a result of the energy crises of the early 2000s. Wars in the Middle East provided OPEC the chance to raise oil prices, reaching a staggering $100 per barrel in 2008, compared to $17 per barrel ten years prior, and $35 only five years before.

So, what has happened since then? With their alliance? With the oil?

The 53,000 barrels that were promised in the year 2000 were only the beginning, as more than 300 trade agreements were signed between Cuba and Venezuela since Chávez took office. That number increased to 115,000 barrels only a few years later, then 400,000 barrels, and up until 2019, 3,000,000 barrels to Cuba... as a gift. In the last seven years, Venezuela gifted Cuba over 50 million dollars in non-commercial agreements. As for the oil that Venezuela gives away to Cuba, the island then resells that oil internationally at market prices. In 2008, Venezuela reached an agreement with China, to which they now owe around 20 billion dollars. The agreement between the countries has allowed Venezuela to receive loans paid for and guaranteed by the Chinese government in exchange for oil. The debt allows Venezuela to keep sending oil to Cuba and simultaneously to China.

The deal with China, however, has not panned out as Chávez expected it to. Since its debt to China now exceeds a quarter of its own GDP, Venezuela is now the country in this hemisphere that owes most to the People's Republic of China. The relationship between the Eastern nation and Venezuela has become undoubtedly strained by Venezuela's economic collapse and the mismanagement of its state-owned oil industry: PDVSA. As a result of the losses, Venezuela has not been able to pay its debts to China, resulting in PDVSA's three largest oil tankers being taken by China. Once a gem when it came to oil production and export, as of 2020, Venezuela is importing oil from Iran. Only time will tell if international pressure leads to any political change.

Let's get back to Cuba, however, because the trade did not stop with oil, although oil has been the driver for more trade. According to the late President Chávez himself, as of 2012, 44,804 Cubans were working in public administration in Venezuela. Today, the figure would be harder to find, given the lack of transparency from the Venezuelan government and their tight grip on information, so for now, let's take Chávez's word. Cubans are now the ones who control the ID system in Venezuela, its registries, and notaries. According to Antonio Rivero, a former general of the Venezuelan armed forces, there are around 100,000 Cubans in Venezuela, and that 20% of them have been trained for war. He notes that they are there to secure the interests of Havana. He stated that over five years ago, there were 3,700 G2 intelligence officers in Venezuela; the number has most likely grown since then. Rivero was one of the first in the military to confront the late President Chávez about the Cuban intrusion. Many like Rivero have now been rooted out of the military and run out of the Venezuelan government.

After Chávez died, there was a question about how that would affect the Cuban economy since the commercial relationship between Cuba and Venezuela at the time accounted for 40% of Cuban trade and 18% of Cuba's gross economic product. Basically, Cuba depends on Venezuela's political condition, and since Chávez died, the situation was unpredictable. The late Hugo Chávez personally chose Nicolás Maduro to be his successor. Maduro has no known education, and his background is shady at best. The current President Maduro spent years in Cuba, and he is the person Chávez trusted the most in his entourage. Many will say Nicolás Maduro is simply a puppet, a puppet who does and says everything the Cuban caudillos command him to. He regularly proves this to be the case by his frequent trips to the island for political consultation. Since he took office, however, he goes through periods of instability and stability; the situation in Venezuela is like that of a rollercoaster, always with a surprise. The first year after he was elected, he experienced countrywide protests that lasted for months and happened again in 2017. According to national polls, over 90% of the country is against his administration. But clearly, disapproval rating won't make any difference. Coincidentally, it was right after the student protest erupted in 2014 that Cuba started opening its doors and began talks with the U.S. to provide a closer relationship with the northern so-called "empire" and the communist island. Leaving the U.S.-hatred speeches behind and bringing Maduro's constant rhetoric against the U.S. to a halt.

The Chavista dialog needs an outside enemy to keep the focus on the outside rather than face the internal reality. The United States and the "oligarchy" have always been the scapegoats of the Venezuelan regime to keep from facing their own inefficiencies and keep the country divided and filled with hatred for one another. Since Cuba was basically controlling Maduro's decisions while the talks between the U.S. and Cuba were going on, Maduro briefly blamed Spain for the problems for a time in 2015. The rhetoric is the same, but the target changed. As mentioned before, the political situation is volatile, and while Cuba maneuvers to try to get a more stable partner, the Venezuelan government will still rely on the island for "good advice." This situation is far from over, but this is when we will see whether a government finally collapses from the weight of its own troubles or manages to rise again from the ashes. That remains to be seen.

V

The 47-Hour Resignation

When Chávez won the presidency in 1998, many of those who did not vote for him supported him as president, for he was to be the leader of our free nation. We, of course, wanted our leader to do well by our country. That's the way it should work in a democracy, right? We hope our leaders will have a successful term and guide our countries into prosperity and growth, regardless of disagreements over policy. However, many of those hopeful people who put their faith in the man who had been voted into office in 1998 began to have serious doubts early on, and many saw serious red flags. According to some polls as early as 2 years after his election, more than half the country already felt anger towards Chávez, who only two years prior, 90% of people were cheering for.

Of course, there were those who never supported him; my parents were part of that group. They saw him as a tyrant, but were hopeful the separation of powers instituted in the nation would keep him from becoming one. There were the pessimists and the optimists. One of my uncles, although he intensely disliked Chávez and believed he was "bad for business," also tried to quell the fears of my parents and other family members early on, saying in 2001, right after Chávez had attempted to institute education reform but had failed, that "we already reached rock bottom," and that in 2001, Venezuela was the worst it could get. Obviously, he was optimistic but wrong in his estimation.

Most people are probably aware that Venezuela is an oil-rich nation. Ideally, we shouldn't be as dependent as we are on oil, but we are. Pro: when things are good, they can get really good, not to mention that gas is dirt cheap for Venezuelans. Con: in the wrong hands, oil money becomes a great incentive for corruption. Oil reserves are a double-edged sword — a blessing and a curse. Chávez said he wanted to make Venezuela economically independent, as had many leaders of the past. So, he went for the country's golden goose: PDVSA, or Petroleum of Venezuela. The company had already been nationalized years prior. However, Chávez wanted to make sure he was in better control of its operations, therefore in late 2001, he named his allies to the company board, fired some senior executives, and made sure some of his generals and academics had influence over the company, even though many of them had no experience in the business.

This move, of course, inspired a backlash, as many of the company's top people had been there for decades. Suddenly, growing party lines were noticeable within PDVSA.

Simultaneously, opposition to Chávez was growing in civil society and within other industries. Disapproval to Chávez started growing stronger by late 2001 when Chávez passed 49 new laws concerning the economy through a presidential decree. The organization known as FEDECAMARAS (the leading business association in the country) began demonstrating their opposition to the new laws and the Chávez administration. The country's largest union organization (CTV) also showed their discontent by joining FEDECAMARAS and PDVSA workers in a one-day peaceful protest. Their complaint pointed out the worsening economic conditions in the country, thereby further polarizing society. Opposition students also held protests on university campuses against President Chávez. On the 21st of February, while the press was also capturing their discontent, Chávez sympathizers, otherwise known as "Chavistas," showed up at the students' protest with sticks and stones ready to physically show their repudiation of the opposition youth movement. Several people, including members of the press, were injured. Polarization would only grow worse from here.

On the 9th of April, due to the obvious division and staunch opposition to Chávez, FEDECAMARAS, the CTV, and political opposition to Chávez called for a general strike. Because PDVSA wanted Chávez to stop meddling in the company, the oil organization also joined the call for a strike on April 11th. Tension grew, and apart from thousands upon thousands of members of said organizations, the civil society also joined a massive protest on that day. Hundreds of thousands of people filled the streets. My parents went, my older cousins went, my friends' parents went, uncles, sisters, and brothers of people I knew were there. My parents showed up wearing running shoes, baseball caps, and comforta-ble outfits so they would be able to stand in the sunlight for hours, and of course, like many others, they held a flag. They took my dad's aunt and a family friend.

It seemed like a day full of hope, with at least half a million people present. Those of us who stayed at home because we were too young to even know what was happening, much less be able to participate, could see the colors of our flag sprawled across our television screen as the news reported the ongoing massive rally. The speakers passionately called for a change, for they believed this government did not care about the people's interests. With the crowd's intensity and seeing the strength in their numbers, they began calling for Chávez's resignation. The crowd's support emboldened its leaders, so they started making their way towards Miraflores, the house where the president worked, to demand Chávez step down that same day.

You better believe Chávez was watching; in fact, there are those who believe he had a plan in place for the opposition. During the protest, we could see the civilians marching through the streets on our TV screens, and in a moment, Chávez's face replaced the images. In his typical entertainer's fashion, he started addressing the nation. Those of us who were watching from home could no longer see the protest — only him. *What was he talking about?* He was saying nothing of importance. Some said he was sending en-crypted messages; others believed it was merely a distraction to keep the public from seeing the mass of people coming to ask for his resignation. One TV station decided to broadcast the protest and split the screen between Chávez and what was happening in Caracas. The contrast made Chávez look like a liar. This decision by the TV station would cost them later on, but at the time, those watching the TV screen could see the glaring reality, in contrast to a fantasy Chávez seemed to be selling.

Not long after that, leaked recordings came out of Chávez commanding the military to deploy and repress the unarmed protesters. The protesters were so peaceful that they even stopped at red lights to allow cars to pass, yet they kept marching. The military, however, refused Chávez's commands. They refused to unleash the tanks because they believed that would not be in the people's interests — the people were exercising their constitutional rights. The generals believed there would be a massive number of casualties and violence given the number of people present if they did. The military's refusal did not prevent violence against the protestors, as other people were ready to take things into their own hands. As people marched on towards Miraflores, a group of government sympathizers made their way to confront the opposition members; chaos was about to erupt.

Apart from the "Chavistas" making their way to confront the marchers, suddenly, the crowd began to hear screams. Shots were being fired near the front of the protest. My father distinctly remembers having a gut feeling a moment before as they approached the front. He saw his aunt walking in front of him and had a sudden impulse to grab her by the arm and tell her to pull back. So, they started lagging to the back while letting dozens of people pass them. His hunch was correct. Soon the screams grew louder, the crowds began to panic, people started running in all directions, not knowing where the shots were coming from. They headed to the car and decided to drive back. Then they got a phone call from my uncle on my mother's side. He asked if they were still there; he was calling to warn them that there were shooters on the rooftops, he was able to see them on the one TV channel broadcasting live. Snipers in civilian clothing were perched on the sides of the bridge and the buildings that the protesters were walking under. They had opened fire on a crowd of unarmed civilians. Some police were ordered to stand down, while others were ordered to defend the civilians. Those who issued the latter order would later be prosecuted and blamed for the casualties that resulted on that day.

Rumor has it that some of the civilians who fired at the gathered opposition were collaborating with Chávez and his government. Chaos was rampant. The result was that 18 civilians were killed, including a press photographer covering the event, and 150 people were injured. Immediately after these events, a group of high-ranking military officials went to Chávez and demanded his resignation. It is important to note that this was not the first time the military has asked Chávez for his resignation. Some members had done this a couple of months before in February. On April 11th, in the aftermath of the protest, Chávez went on national TV once again, but this time it was to announce that he was "abandoning his duties" as president of the Republic. He then was exiled for 47 hours. There were rumors about escapes to Caribbean islands, including "La Orchila," where there is a presidential retreat. There were calls to and from Cuba, the military chain of command collapsed. Chávez's right hand and most trusted military aid informed the public of the president's official resignation. To this day, however, we are not sure if Chávez signed an official document resigning the office of the president.

Chávez had abandoned his duties and allegedly gone to La Orchila, a military base off the coast of Venezuela, and so the opposition declared itself triumphant. Pedro Carmona Estanga, the president of the organization of FEDECAMARAS, briefly assumed the presidency. He was president for the weekend, intending to call for new elections and elect a new president. I remember that weekend, we had a family get-together, my cousins on my dad's side of the family were there, and even though we were too young to understand, there was a sense of relief coming from the adults in the room. I remember my mother saying to my aunt that we had just avoided the country's potential destruction at the hands of a communist and that we were now free. Of course, I had been hearing about Chávez and his government for years, and this development seemed very good to a preteen's limited understanding. I just didn't quite understand the depth of the issue. But I, too, felt a sense of relief. Little did we know, there was much going on behinds the scenes, something that would cut our respite short.

We began to hear of violence throughout the poorest areas of Caracas, where people were demanding that Chávez be reinstated. There was rioting and looting, people were shot and assaulted, and some members of the military started feeling immense pressure to reinstate the banished president. Other things were going on, conversations between the Venezuelan military and the Cuban government. What were the conversations? We have yet to find out, but it was enough for Chávez to come back after two days. Because of pressure from the military and the Chavista civilians, the Carmona government collapsed, and Chávez was reinstated on the 14th of April 2002. Of course, there were many who said this was a U.S. coup, and I couldn't tell you how much of that is reality. I have never seen evidence of that; however, I can tell you that a vast number of Venezuelans wanted Chávez out. Unfortunately, that was not to be the case. Chavista supporters demanded retribution, some even calling for death to those officers who helped in the brief toppling of Chávez. However, it would be hypocritical for Chávez and his people to call for such a consequence, given Chávez's own, more violent history with coup attempts. But being hypocritical does not seem to matter, once you are in power, your own standards do not apply to your own actions, or so it seems.

After this effort to unseat him from office, the dialogue between the opposition and the government broke down further. Polarization accelerated, and Chávez was not looking to bridge the gap nor heal the nation. His government even blamed the violence of the 11th of April on the opposition and created the idea that the victims were his sympathizers.

It is like the two sides were living in alternate realities.

By the fall of that year, only four people had been arrested for the violent events of April 11th. The people were losing faith when it came to our country's ability to prosecute criminals. After that day, Chávez radicalized his rhetoric even further, getting more and more aggressive against anyone who opposed him, degrading the civilians who opposed him, and incentivizing violence towards any news media that showed tendencies against him. His language had previously galvanized his supporters to attack the press. Many journalists reported that they had started receiving threats and sometimes were physically assaulted by "Chavistas." Only a few months after April 11th, after Chávez had ramped up his aggressiveness against the press, someone threw a hand grenade at the news channel building of Globovision. Things were about to get rough for the free press in Venezuela. That year, at least 25 journalists requested precautionary measures from the Inter-American Commission of Human Rights.

However, the opposition, both civilian and political, kept trying to find ways to remove President Chávez by legal means. Protests continued throughout the summer. Parents would attend neighborhood meetings to pitch ideas and find a way out of what we saw as a looming dictatorship; there were continuous grassroots efforts. After all, Chávez had announced that same summer that he wanted to reform the Venezuelan Carta Magna again.

As a consequence of the April 11th protests, the government found ways to quash dissent while making their decisions seem democratic to the rest of the world. After April 11th, the government instituted more obstacles against peaceful protests, more ways to criminalize peaceful assembly, and created exclusion zones to impede any kind of gathering. Barriers were built to prevent any protests from reaching governmental institutions, such as Miraflores, the National Assembly, and other smaller institutions. The logic behind creating barriers, both physically and with laws, seemed to go beyond merely hindering political dissent — it also seemed like a way to plant the idea in the populace that any demonstration that had as its destination the main government headquarters of the country, had the purpose of generating chaos and promoting a coup d'état.

Not very different from how the U.S. government reacted and built barriers around the Capitol building in Washington, D.C. Hence, any repressive and authoritarian response against the opposition was justified. Despite the extensive constitutional and legal protection that the right to peaceful assembly and demonstration has in Venezuela, laws have been approved and reformed that restrict the right to demonstrate. When widely interpreted by the Justice Administration System, they are applied to people who exercise their rights peacefully. What's one to take from that? That despite systems and laws and the Carta Magna being in place, those who administer them are still susceptible to influence and bias. Just because there is a separation of power does not mean that system cannot fail.

Between 2005 and 2013, at least 150 union leaders became the victims of political prosecution and/or imprisonment. The justification was always for "the common good" or the "defense of the interests of the nation." But really, it was the defense of the ideology and government of Chávez. After 2002, every cycle of significant protests has had, as a direct or indirect consequence, suppression by the use of government institutions and the oppressive use of excessive force to punish. Don't ever think that tyranny happens from one day to the next; it is a progression. Tyrants do not arrive waving the flag; they slowly but surely remove individual rights. In hindsight, many ask, how did people not fight this? Well, they did.

To this day, what happened on April 11th is used as leverage by the Chavista supporters who claim the opposition was undemocratic for staging a coup against the president. For the opposition, however, the date is a day to remember the victims who have not received justice. There is a belief by many in the opposition that it was Fidel Castro who orchestrated Chávez's comeback by convincing him and other members of the military to reinstate him. Because of that, the speculation is that Chávez remained forever grateful to the communist leader and was determined to repay him for his help. The idea wouldn't be too much of a stretch, considering the seeming merger between the countries after the fact.

VI
The 2002 Oil Lockout

It was the start of December 2002, and it had been quite a year. At this point, it seemed normal to have your family go to protest after protest, political meeting after political meeting. It was just our way of life between going to school, family gatherings on the weekends, and getting ready for my first communion. 2002 had been, in a way, as hectic a year as could be for a third-grader, and the political situation was always in the background. It was almost like a game.

Every year, the most important theater in Venezuela, the Teresa Carreño Theater, put on a traditional show for Christmas, The Nutcracker. My family and I went every single year. Even though I almost knew the show by heart, I could not get enough of watching the dancers and enjoying the Christmas scene. I would often run into school friends in the audience, and my parents would run into family friends. Overall, it simply felt like a joyful and peaceful atmosphere.

This particular year, during the ballet's intermission, a man came out on stage wearing a fabulous white silk suit; he looked as if he had walked straight of Louis XIV's Court. He treated the audience to some storytelling and anecdotes, wishing everyone a Merry Christmas and a Happy New Year. However, what I will never forget was his reference to politics, his confidence in what was to come, and his encouragement, telling us all to participate in the coming general national strike. I'm not sure now that everyone was pleased with him saying so, but he seemed comfortable enough to say it. As far as I was concerned, the general strike meant I would have a few days off school. That was good enough for me!

The reality was, in fact, a lot more complex. The strike, which was called for by FEDECAMARAS and the National Union Association of Workers (CTV), resulted from more than a year of challenging protests, a year with temporary presidential removal, and a year of political violence. In November 2000, the National Assembly, with a "Chavista" majority, gave special powers to President Chávez, allowing him to rule by decree. So, he was able to fast-track the passage of a set of economic laws that fit his political ideologies and goals. These new laws basically imposed harsh regulations on various industries, such as manufacturing, fishing, and the oil industry, which slowed down and limited production capacity. His rulings also raised the taxes. None of the measures were welcomed by the commercial class, which promptly began to voice their concerns and ask for a free market approach. This move by Chávez essentially lost him backing, even from some of his own allies who had supported him through his election and had become his political advisors. One of them was Luis Miquelena, who had been involved in Venezuelan politics since the 1940s as an old-school progressive. Miquelena urged Chávez not to take such harsh economic measures but eventually moved away from him and his cabinet as he realized he could not control Chávez. This is what happened to much of the old Venezuelan political class, which had supported Chávez early on, thinking they could mold him and shape him, given his naiveté and political inexperience. Obviously, they quickly discovered how wrong they had been to prop him up, and they would eventually admit to their complicity in helping the country fall into the abyss.

The general strike started on the second of December 2002. The call for various industries to join was supported by the board of PDVSA (Venezuela's national oil industry) and its management-level employees. The country was about to become paralyzed. Most private schools joined the call, stores were closed, sporting and entertainment events were halted, supermarkets reduced their hours, and commercial manufacturing shut down. Many small businesses that did not want to join the strike had no other option. It was right before Christmas, and after a few days of the country being in lockdown, my parents decided to go abroad. So, we boarded a plane and were able to spend the rest of the strike abroad. For me, this was a vacation, so I was one of the lucky ones. For many, it was torturous and isolating. It became a strike with no defined end date; the opposition demanded the recall of the president's new laws and a return to a free-market approach, but eventually, they simply demanded Chávez's resignation. The only services left working were the water, electricity, and communication services, as well as private and state media.

A few days into the strike, Altamira Plaza in Caracas became a gathering center for the opposition. Thousands would gather daily to join and listen to the speakers, ranging from military officials in the resistance, opposition political leaders, artists, journalists, and industry leaders. It was a point of motivation; it was a point of hope for many people. Private news organizations had decided to primarily inform the public about the strike and abandon their regular programming. Cameras were stationed at Altamira Plaza 24/7, and they were capturing every moment, the slow nights and the active days. On the 5th night of gathering in the Plaza, at around 9 pm, a shooting took place. A person approached the group and fired 20 times into the crowd, leaving 3 dead and 13 people injured. The news media captured everything, and soon they were playing clips of the violence over and over on their TV screens.

Over the next few days, the protests intensified as a response to the violence. People were angry, and it became a stronger point of pressure for the Chavista government. It seemed that the government would collapse under the pressure. The opposition, at this point, was determined in their demands; they would not back down, but neither would Chávez. There was no point of compromise. The polarization was already there among the general population, but the paralyzing of society seemed to be exacerbating the division. The civilian community that opposed the government saw the strike and the paralyzation of society as a necessary evil, which would cause temporary damage economically. This seemed better than the alternative of the long-term damage Chávez could cause with his policies — the opposition simply saw the strike as civil disobedience. The everyday citizens who agreed with the government saw the strike as an attack on them and those they supported. They called the strike an "oil coup," so their support for Chávez, in many ways, was strengthened. The government sympathizers even took to the streets to protest against the news outlets covering the opposition strikes 24/7, thereby taking away any other programs.

People were fighting amongst themselves; friends could hardly find common ground anymore. Families with different political opinions would ex-communicate each other. There were many, of course, lucky family units who, for the most part, shared values and ideologies, and therefore shared their political affiliation. In the past, many members of society voted for different political groups, but those old-school parties were now barely even mentioned. They might have opposed each other in the past, but in the new era of Chávez, they formed a coalition against him, for his was a completely different style of politics. This leftist, populist style, which claimed to be for the people, mainly created a new kind of elite corrupt political class intent on crushing any new type of wealth creation that didn't benefit them directly. Of course, that was not Chávez's official position, but it was the clear end result of his policies.

At the beginning of the strike, the government attempted to deny there was anything of importance going on. They especially wanted to pretend that everything was working just as usual when it came to PDVSA, the oil industry. Soon enough, however, it became very evident that was not the case. On the first week of the strike, the crew of one of the country's essential oil tankers, "Pilin Leon," declared a rebellion and anchored the ship in Lake Maracaibo. Soon other tankers — which were meant to transport oil from refineries or to other countries — followed their example. For a country that produced oil and sold it to its citizens cheaper than water, this was a big deal. Soon enough, the fifth largest producer of oil in the world now had to import oil from Brazil and other nations to keep up with demand. Venezuelans were used to an abundance of gasoline, to the point that it felt like citizens were being paid to drive. In fact, at that time, cars were not generally assets that would depreciate in value over time. In most cases, you could sell your car at the same price as you bought it years before.

Oil money dictated the behavior of the average Venezuelan, and we became a population of fast consumers, just like the government. When Venezuela saw an increase in oil revenue, the government spent lavishly on public resources; when we saw a downswing, those same public resources would weaken. The average person didn't accumulate wealth but spent their money on fast goods. The behavior of the president seemed to shape the spending behavior of millions. The screeching halt in oil revenue showed the lack of long-term planning by many average citizens and the government they had elected.

The imported gas was barely enough. Venezuelan gas stations ran out of fuel, there were long lines daily, and people started rationing their gas like never before. Crude exports fell to a trickle and caused the country to lose billions of dollars in business. Seeing the value of their currency dropping, many Venezuelans started turning their currency into hard money deposits overseas. Chávez reacted by imposing harsher regulations to prevent money from leaving the country. So CADIVI was born, an exchange system that attempted to fix the foreign exchange rate. However, this eventually caused the black market to become commonplace for the middle and upper classes to trade money. During the national strike, the opposition kept protesting, whether by going to the Altamira Plaza, going to various marches around the country, or participating in the nightly cacerolazos.* My family stayed abroad through the holidays; my brothers and I were enrolled in school temporarily. We would get daily updates from

* A *cacerolazo* essentially means: a form of popular protest which consists of a group of people making noise by banging pots, pans, and other utensils in order to call for attention. The first documented protests of this style occurred in France in the 1830s.

family members who had remained in Caracas and who, as they said, barely left their homes anymore except for visiting each other.

So, what was to happen? No side was compromising, and something had to change. The opposition within PDVSA became more entrenched through the weeks; the higher-ups saw Chávez as a threat to their system. They believed Chávez was attempting to gain total control of the industry. Even if it was a national company, the organization directive still maintained the power of decision. President Chávez wanted to change that. The president argued that he simply wanted to get rid of the high spending, as he believed it was unnecessary and that he could change the industry into becoming more efficient while also redirecting PDVSA to work for the "social good." Middle management was entrenched in their fight against Chávez. They didn't believe in the president's "good intentions." They believed Chávez was attempting to politicize the industry and get rid of meritocracy or promotion by merit.

Obviously, Chávez's government didn't fall this time. No one budged, neither the opposition nor the government, but whichever side failed in their goal would suffer harsh consequences. This time it was the opposition. The strike started failing when there were small chinks in the armor of the plan. The first symptom that the government would regain control occurred on December 21st when the employees loyal to the government managed to regain control of the first oil tanker to be stopped by the resistance: Pilin Leon. Some PDVSA employees volunteered to keep the company going, so they went against the plan of the other employees and upper management. Local businesses grew tired of the standstill and disobeyed the national unions. Many began to reopen their businesses, giving some breathing room to the government. But there was still over a month of paralysis left.

However, the most significant blow to the opposition's plan came from a man named Wilmer Ruperti, a Venezuelan entrepreneur and businessman who saw an opportunity to increase his wealth. Ruperti had some Russian contacts, which he leveraged to break the oil blockade. He moved quickly, created a shell company with the name of PDVSA, which caused a Russian company to believe that they were dealing directly with the official Venezuelan company. Therefore, he was able to charter Russian tankers and bring fuel to Venezuela by selling that oil to the South American government. Ruperti exploited the situation by utilizing his relationships with Venezuelan officials and his Russian contacts. In 2006, in an email to one of the Chávez brothers, he explains what happened:

> The Russian ships were the ones who broke the naval blockade that took place in the country in December 2002. In a meeting at the Miraflores Palace with the military high command and then with Mr. Ali Rodriguez Araque and Mr. Rafael Ramirez, I decided to break this blockade. At the time, I made it clear that the Russian fleet could succeed in breaking the blockade, and they allowed me to

charter, together with the chartering desk, all the vessels that I could... the only drawback with the Russians was the way they guarantee payment of their freight and in a meeting at PDVSA, in their own offices, under the pseudonym of Captain Fausto, Mr. Ali Rodriguez Araque and to the contingency authorized me to carry out the transaction...

How did Ruperti do it? He chartered ships from the Russian company Novoship UK Ltd. Using his contact, a corrupt Russian staff member who managed to make his company believe that the shell companies Ruperti had set up were the legitimate Venezuelan companies, Novoship chartered their ships to Ruperti's companies. In turn, Ruperti chartered the vessels to the Chavista government. The way Ruperti did this was quite blunt — he would use a Panamanian shell company, called PDVSA Marketing International Trading (PMI Trading), in negotiations with Novoship. His plan worked perfectly, and the Chavistas viewed his intervention as crucial to end the strike. His quick thinking during the crisis netted him a lofty 16 million dollars. Nowadays, Ruperti is living the good life, except for the fact that many in the opposition know him and shun him. Overall, he says he made the right choice. Only a few years later, in 2008, Ruperti's business owned over 15 ships and became worth over a billion dollars. His aid to President Chávez and his "socialist revolution" also garnered him the favor of the president, meaning that many times after the fact, Ruperti served as a consultant for his business expertise of

PDVSA, after Chávez had fired most of the experts for defying him. Ruperti now travels in private jets, travels around in armored cars, and is constantly accompanied by Korean bodyguards. In an interview in 2006 with the *Wall Street Journal*, Ruperti said, "A lot of people think I'm a devil, but it's not true... I sleep well at night, and I'm morally satisfied."

Well, Ruperti made his fortune on that strike, but many business professionals met their demise. After the strike ended on February 2nd, the opposition quickly thought of another way to find freedom from Chávez's government — through a constitutional call for a referendum that allowed the citizens to recall Chávez if there was enough support for his removal. Just before the strike ended, the opposition went to work collecting the signatures, which were eventually rejected by the National Electoral Council because of legal technicalities, but they would try again. However, because the strike ended, many of the leaders who supported it had to leave the country for fear of prosecution, especially industry leaders who were part of FEDECAMARAS.

Chávez became even more radicalized after the 2-month paralysis of the country. As you remember, he was attempting to gain control of PDVSA, and it was upper and middle management who defied him. Chávez, with his typical showmanship style, fired oil executives while announcing their names on national TV and blowing a whistle like a referee. I remember that this was when the first wave of middle-class and upper-class Venezuelans began to leave the country by the thousands. This was the first time I had friends announcing in school that they would not be here next year because their parents had decided to leave. This was when my cousins made use of their dual Venezuelan-Spanish nationality and set off for Spain, not because they were connected to PDVSA, but because they perceived the country's future to be bleak. The PDVSA strike had highlighted that possibility. But many of us believed, like my parents, that this storm would pass soon enough. During this PDVSA purge, Chávez also ousted more than 19 thousand employees from the company because he deemed them to be enemies of the state for abandoning their posts and boycotting the industry. Technically, one could think he was justified in doing so; the problem was how he went about it. PDVSA had set up oil fields with homes for their workers, Chávez sent the military in the middle of the night, with tear gas, and tore men, women, and children out of their homes, and put them out on the street with nowhere to go. This was his punishment for acting against him.

The strike was a risk, and it didn't pay off for the opposition or for the country's population and economy. The consequences were felt mostly by the middle and lower classes. Because private industry had essentially been shut down for two months, they had to take measures to keep afloat, so they cut hours and personnel, thereby contributing to the nation's unemployment, which only grew after the strike. There was a scarcity of food for some time, and many companies filed for bankruptcy. The political consequences were also severe for the opposition movement. As I

mentioned, some of the industry leaders left the country. Specifically, Carlos Ortega, and Carlos Fernández, the presidents of the
CTV and FEDECAMARAS, respectively, both charged with the
crimes of treason and civil rebellion. Both are now living in exile,
barely escaping the sentencing of the government. Because of the
strike, Chávez had the perfect excuse to take over PDVSA, fire the
people who were not his loyal followers, and put in those who
were loyal to party politics, regardless of their levels of expertise.
The result: the company's culture changed, favoring politics over
production. Even the PDVSA logo changed, to the Chavista party
color of red, to signal the arrival of a socialist bent. Employees
were given red shirts as the new uniform, and wearing political
gear in favor of Chávez and the socialist movement was encouraged. It also became mandatory for all PDVSA employees to attend political meetings, especially board members, managers, and
PDVSA's president, who could be spotted at Chávez's nationally
televised events where the president would speak for several
hours. When top PDVSA executives failed to show up to Chávez's
televised events and instead chose to work, Chávez would scold
them on national television.

Now, what was the result for PDVSA when it came to its out-
put? Did it really get more efficient after his leadership? Well, let's
look at the facts. Venezuela is sitting on the world's largest oil re-
serve, but it cannot produce enough oil, so ironically, they are
now, as I write this in 2020, importing oil from Iran. Could it have
something to do with the mismanagement of the industry 18 years

ago? Perhaps the firing of its experts who went on to work in other oil industries around the world? Perhaps. Let's take it back to 2016, just three years after Chávez died, and his influence was still present. In 2016, the company was producing nearly one-fifth less than it produced in 1999. Obviously, Chávez making promises of a more efficient PDVSA was all talk. PDVSA is not efficient; it has a bloated bureaucracy, which has about twice the number of people employed by Exxon, despite Exxon producing 66% more oil than Venezuela. Here is proof of what we already know; governments generally are not more efficient at producing goods than the free market. But let's not just blame regular government inefficiencies here; the state oil company, Saudi Aramco, employs less than half the number of people that work for PDVSA and produces more than 3½ times what the South American country produces. Obviously, Chávez and his political heir, Nicolás Maduro, have made a disaster of our oil industry. In 1999, Chávez auctioned 23 state-owned jets because he vowed his government would never abuse the privileges of government planes. Unfortunately, that was another empty promise. PDVSA's company planes have become taxis for company executives, their families, and friends, who take leisure trips to places like Sydney, Hawaii, Paris, and anywhere else they please. Chávez also lent the planes to political allies in the region. How did your promise to end corruption work out for you, Mr. President?

VII

The Year of the Signatures

I remember many times during the early 2000s, my parents going off to different neighborhood association meetings to engage in political activism. Listening to the radio on my way to school and back would inform me of the country's situation and what various political analysts, academics, and pundits of the opposition saw as the way forward. I even remember several occasions when my brothers and I would be spending time with my grandparents. As the clock struck 7, or 8, or whatever it was programmed that day, my grandparents would get up with pots and pans, go into the yard, and bang them together. It sounds kind of funny as I write this now, but what we call the "cacerolazo" was (and still is) a legitimate form of protest where at a specific time of day or evening, people of the opposition all over the country would gather in their balconies, front door, or yard, and bang kitchenware to make noise "waves" through the city. Even if you didn't know there was a protest going on, the sound would certainly let everyone know the amount of discontent we were experiencing.

We had a two-day respite in 2002 where the opposition thought the spirit of freedom had won; the spirit of what we always thought was a characteristic of the Venezuelan people; given the birth of our nation. After that day, when the military was pressured into bringing Hugo Chávez back into office and return him from his exile in Cuba, all the opposition could do, was pick itself back up and keep up the fight, and so, they did. Following that protest, people kept gathering throughout the country's streets; people kept protesting throughout the summer and fall of 2002. They protested by marching, they protested by civil disobedience, and they organized large-scale "cacerolazos." Simultaneously, Chávez promoted his own gatherings in his support. Of course, the crowds were much smaller, and many times he had to send buses out into rural areas to bring in supporters for the counter-protests, but these gatherings only exacerbated further the polarization, as many opposition members were often physically bullied by Chávez sympathizers, and the opposition mostly left the Chavista gatherings alone. That summer of 2002, on July 5th, the group "Coordinadora Democrática" (Democratic Coordinator, CD) was created as an umbrella organization to forge an alliance of various opposition groups and parties. Apart from organizing the general oil strike of 2002-2003, they also took the lead in the effort to call for a referendum to recall Chávez as president.

It was apparent that a large part of the population wanted Chávez to leave. There was a constitutional way to have the citizens

remove him from office by voting, even before the next presidential election. In 2003, a group of organizations, including
FEDECAMARAS, CTV, and the Catholic Church in Venezuela,
joined together to find a way out. They found one. At least a way
to remove the president in a constitutional manner before the end
of his first term. There was a genuine fear that Chávez was there
to stay for life, become a tyrant, and destroy the nation if he was
allowed any time to cement his power. Throughout 2003 and
2004, Coordinadora Democrática worked to collect signatures for
a presidential recall by the opposition. The petition was backed
by Article 72 of the Venezuelan Carta Magna, which states: "All
magistrates and other offices filled by popular vote are subject to
revocation. Once half of the term of office to which an official has
been elected has elapsed, a number of voters constituting at least
20% of the voters registered in the pertinent circumscription may
extend a petition for the calling of a referendum to revoke such
official's mandate. When a number of voters equal to or greater
than the number of those who elected the official vote in favor of
revocation, provided that a number of voters equal to or greater
than 25% of the total number of registered voters have voted in
the recall election, the official's mandate shall be deemed revoked,
and immediate action shall be taken to fill the permanent vacancy
as provided for by this Constitution and by law."

Because of this article, the opposition had found a constitutional and democratic path to remove Chávez from office, and so
they needed to gather at least 2.4 million signatures. Otherwise,

they would have to wait until the next presidential election of 2006. The leaders of CD told the nation that they needed to get ready for the most significant political mobilization in the country in modern times and that this may be the culmination of a civil fight that had been going on for too long. Imagine that if the opposition had said that in 2002, they would not have believed the next two decades would bring the nation to its knees the way they have. Regardless, they were advising citizens to fight against a government that "had failed." One of the promoters of the movement for collecting signatures was Enrique Mendoza, the governor of the state of Miranda. He had said that the gathering of signatures was the culmination of the opposition's struggle within the democratic framework and that he was sure it would be victorious.

Chavistas had a thing for mirroring the opposition in all that they did. When the opposition gathered in protest, they would gather in counter-protest. When the opposition mobilized to collect signatures for the removal of political leaders, so did they. In this case, of course, they didn't collect signatures to remove President Chávez, but for the removal of various opposition leaders within different governmental bodies. The Organization of American States (OAS) and the Carter Center described the Chavista process of gathering signatures as "exemplary" since the process went on without any instances of confrontation or violence from those who disagreed with the movement, namely the opposition.

These organizations then requested the same when it came to collecting signatures on the part of the opposition. However, the Chavista process seemed almost for show, given that it never amounted to anything significant, except that the sympathizers of Chávez managed to do what they wanted in the National Assembly due to their lack of respect for the Constitution. However, the gathering of signatures by the opposition did not go on without a hitch; many had to deal with violence, confrontation, and harassment by government sympathizers, to the point of people being physically attacked and injured.

While the diverse collection of signatures went on, Chávez was confidently (at least in appearance) saying that it was impossible for the opposition to get the signatures they needed to initiate the process for a recall, which they had tried on multiple occasions since the start of this process at the end of 2002. However, the National Electoral Council (CNE) kept putting up obstacles and rejecting their attempts. On one occasion, the opposition claimed to have gathered over 4 million signatures on February 2nd, 2003, which was a higher number than even Chávez had received when he won election in 1998. The opposition movement was collecting signatures by setting up various centers around the country in public spaces where people could go to put their names down. Around 3,200 signing places were set up for the public. There were also canvassers working hard, going door to door, trying to get as many signatures as possible. My parents, of course, participated . They would even drive my great-grandmother and my great-aunt to these centers because these ladies, despite having health issues that would often have them stuck at home, felt it was imperative to take part in this important democratic process. The signatures were not only needed to revoke Chávez's presidency but to disavow his rule and presidential decrees.

That collection of signatures in February was rejected on technicalities, so the opposition was at work again, and by August 2003, they had collected 3.2 million signatures. They were also rejected by the CNE based on the technicality that the signatures had been collected before the middle of the presidential term. In November of that same year, they presented 3.6 million signatures. The organization in charge of gathering the signatures, "Sumate," recognized that probably 8% of them were invalid, but that was well within the margin of error given that they only needed 2.4 million to start the process of the referendum. However, the CNE rejected the signatures on the claim that 1.9 million of them were invalid. It may be important to note that the CNE was a governmental body; it was not really an independent institution, at least not how it was meant to be.

During this process, even a foreign magazine wrote a piece pointing out how Chávez was filling positions within the CNE with his own people. It seemed as if Chávez was using the obstacles to buy himself time, stuff his own people into the Electoral Council, and make sure a system was in place so that he was certain to win the vote when the referendum was finally activated.

The decision by the CNE to reject the signatures and, therefore, further delay the process resulted in massive protests. On occasion, these would turn violent because of confrontations with various groups, resulting in deaths, injuries, and arrests. This rejection by the CNE was appealed and taken to the Electoral Chamber of the Supreme Court of Justice. The Court ruled that the CNE should include 800 thousand of the signatures they had rejected, therefore giving the opposition of total of 2.7 million signatures. This amounted to 300 thousand more signatures than they needed to begin the referendum. However, a week later, the Constitutional Chamber of the same court rejected the Electoral Chamber's decision by ruling it had acted outside its jurisdiction. This back and forth, in hindsight, probably showed Chávez where he had a weakness and where he had to change some judges and "pack the Court," which he eventually did. It also allowed the government some room to maneuver and stall. They knew the opposition was relentless and determined and that, ultimately, they would get the referendum. Still, of course, President Chávez wanted to make sure he was ready.

The opposition kept exceeding the expectations set forth by Hugo Chávez in demonstrating that they were, in fact, capable of getting the number of signatures they needed, regardless of the setbacks. Chávez, on his weekly TV talk show (yes, he had one!) called "Aló, Presidente," meaning, "Hello, President" said that the opposition was not legally able to procure the signatures needed and that they were acting in a "fascist, and terrorist" way.

One of the leaders of the Democratic Coordinator organization confidently said that the president was allowed to throw his tantrum, but that they would eventually be victorious. César Gaviria, then the Secretary-General of the OAS, had the Venezuelan president publicly oppose and argue with him when the OAS official declared that the opposition was going through the process legally and that he didn't observe any kind of fraud that the president was suggesting. It may be my own personal observation, but it's often the ones making preliminary accusations that are actually committing the crime. Chávez heavily criticized Gaviria and even claimed that the OAS Secretary was compromised and biased in favor of the Venezuelan opposition.

Following these events, the president tasked a government official with the mission of compiling a list of the names of people who had signed against him. Given this order, the names of the people who signed asking for a referendum became public on a list dubbed "Lista Tascón" (The Tascón List), named after the man tasked to create the list. The president of the National Union Association made a declaration to the Associated Press regarding the list, saying that those on the list had begun to be targeted and that public workers were being fired from their government jobs. The Minister of Health, Roger Capella, also spoke to AP, saying that "everyone that had signed to activate the referendum against President Chávez should be fired from the Ministry of Health." He also noted that signing was "an act of terrorism." His statements caused a major PR backlash for the government, so Mr. Capella withdrew his statement a few days later, noting that firing people for their political leanings was his own personal opinion, not an official policy. What a relief, right?

To correct this impasse by a government official and the PR nightmare this was for the government, the CNE agreed to quell the anger by allowing a period of 5 days for those people whose signatures were being questioned, to rectify any issues and verify their authenticity. The signatures had all been collected with a fingerprint, an ID number, and a signature. It was a difficult process to fake manually, given that all Venezuelans needed to correctly show and give their ID in order for their vote and signature to be counted. However, those were the obstacles that were placed and the cards that were dealt. The opposition was confident that sooner or later they would force the government's hand to allow for the referendum. At the end of the 5-day period, there were finally enough signatures to initiate the referendum. Perhaps the only reason it was allowed to finally take place was that President Chávez himself allowed it since he had now prepared himself and the country for another vote, as he had just recently given a contract to an unknown voting company by the name of Smartmatic to modernize Venezuela's voting system, from a vote that was tabulated manually, to a vote that was to be electronically tabulated.

The day to cast our vote finally arrived on the 15th of August 2004, practically two years after efforts had been started for this process. The opposition requested that their option be the option of YES, which meant "yes, the presidency should be recalled." On the other hand, the option of voting NO meant the rejection of the referendum and that Chávez remained in office. On that day, hundreds of thousands swarmed voting places around the city and even around the world. There were insanely long lines, to the point that the closing hour of the polls had to be extended from 6 pm to midnight, as people claimed their right for their voices to be heard. The process was long, and it took all night until the early hours of the morning. I had gone to sleep, but many had their eyes glued to their TV sets, waiting for the CNE to announce the results. The opposition, after all the trials and tribulations, was confident of their victory. However, some were suspicious of the system installed by Smartmatic right before the election because of the government's claim that it wanted to "modernize" the system and make it more efficient. Finally, at 4am, the CNE announced the results. 94% of the vote had been counted, and the nation heard it had gone to NO with 58% of the vote. Chávez was to remain. It was a huge gut punch to any civilian who had voted YES, especially to the ones who had put their jobs at risk because of the creation of the Tascón List. It seemed that after that day, Chávez reinforced his position, but the opposition weakened, and the alliance which had been formed among opposition parties through CD eventually dissolved.

Regardless of the official numbers put out by the government, the opposition maintained that there was fraud. Yes, that may sound like the move of a "sore loser," which often happens when one side can't accept the result of an election. However, in this case, there was a reason to question the results. The numbers just didn't add up, and many were certain that the Smartmatic machines were compromised. Tulio Álvarez, a constitutionalist lawyer and representative of CD, published an article* titled "Fraud Against Democracy," which was the work of 40 professionals within various fields of expertise. The publication alleged that there was a "qualitative, continuous, selective, and massive" fraud on the manual procedure of voting and the automated machines. The report focuses on irregularities present during the voting process and through the voting registry; it seemed that a non-existent part of the population had gone to vote that day. Quite the claim! It was discovered that in the automated process, 28% of the vote was manipulated, which meant that members of the National Electoral Council and the company, Smartmatic, were compromised. The group that published the study even concluded that the Smartmatic machines were designed to manipulate the vote. Their accusations meant that under Venezuelan law, the vote had to be null and had to be redone. This however, never took place. It was clear then that the people who were supposed to guard our systems, failed.

---

*https://venezuelanalysis.com/news/694
http://www.urru.org/papers/RRfraude/2004_Oct15_Fraud-Against-Democracy_The-Venezuelan-Case.pdf

The Venezuelan opposition was not alone in their claims; a study published in the *International Statistical Review* which examined the Venezuelan Referendum results published their own assessments. They said that by their own findings "the Venezuelan opposition has statistical evidence to reject the official results given by the CNE. The irregularities detected were observed consistently in numerous voting centers, and the magnitude of the irregularities imply that the official results do not reflect the intention of voters with statistical confidence." The journal went on to note that, "The percentage of irregular certificates of election is between 22.2% and 26.5% of the total; 18% of the voting centers show an irregular voting pattern in their certificates of election, the votes corresponding to this irregularity are around 2,550,000; The resulting estimate, using the unbiased votes as representative of the population for the percentage of YES votes against President Chávez is 56.4% as opposed to the official result of 41%" The conclusion of the authors was that the actual result had been flipped and that 56.4% had actually voted YES, and 41% had voted NO. It was a bold claim, and if so, it was one of the biggest scandals in the Venezuelan democracy, but for years it would be swept under the rug. The results, these statisticians claimed, would have dramatically shifted the destiny of a nation that has been ravaged for over two decades by a corrupt, leftist dictatorship. Perhaps one day, not far from the future the conversation will resurface, as the venom of Smartmatic has infected other nations through Dominion Voting Systems.

It is truly abominable what happened to the nation. If the claims of fraud hold true, which at this point are hard to deny, it's heartbreaking to think about what could have happened had things been different. Starting, of course, with what they did to regular people who exercised their constitutional right to ask for a recall of the president. The list which was collected for taking an opposing position to Chávez ruined many lives. President Hugo Chávez had commissioned one of his government officials to assemble the list out of the database of the CNE. The CNE gave him access to this list that was supposed to be private and protected, and they excused themselves by saying that they were simply checking the signatures to assure they were not falsified. The reality was that the Tascón list was released to the public and used to promote political prosecution of those ordinary citizens who had supported the opposition in their efforts. Those most negatively affected were lower-income Venezuelans and those who worked for the public sector. Citizens like Rocío San Miguel Sosa, Magally Chang Girón, and Thais Coromoto Peña were removed from their jobs, along with many others. People's identities were left out in the open for the entire government apparatus and its fervent sympathizers to dismiss, intimidate, humiliate, and chastise because of their lack of support and commitment to the "Bolivarian Revolution."

Fourteen years later, the Inter-American Court of Human Rights ruled that the list was a case of political prosecution and a violation of human rights. In their ruling, the Court concluded that the treatment of those who had signed the referendum petition was retaliation for having legitimately exercised a constitutionally established right of a political nature. Of course, even if we appreciate the ruling, most reasonable Venezuelans had already come to that conclusion. It didn't take us fourteen years to know that creating such a list blatantly discouraged freedom of expression and instilled fear in anyone who dared speak against the powers-that-be. Perhaps the Court's delay can simply serve as a symbol and reminder that truth will come out, and eventually, maybe, justice might prevail, even if it takes time.

VIII

An Epidemic of Violence

It was a Saturday morning, and I was doing my grocery shopping with my college roommate in Boston. While putting my items through the checkout, I started receiving messages from both of my brothers to call them right away. One of them attempted to FaceTime me, but I simply ignored the call, as I felt I was too busy at the moment. Then one of them just texted me the news, which stopped me dead in my tracks, "Mataron a mi tio" the text read. For a moment, I experienced some cognitive dissonance, and I remember my mind trying to negotiate with reality. I remember having thoughts like "this is not real" or "maybe they just tried to kill him but didn't succeed." I immediately texted back, "Which uncle?" He replied, "Uncle Leo." Truth is, I could not believe it, and I pressed my brother for the truth, "Are you sure?" and "Are you serious?" As soon as I understood this was reality, that in fact, my uncle's life was another life taken in the senseless violence of the city of Caracas, I just went silent. I was standing at the checkout aisle with my roommate, so I finished paying for my groceries and walked off in complete silence. My roommate seemed to understand something was off and didn't ask me anything until hours later when I emerged from my room, where I had locked myself away. The truth was, I knew this type of criminality was touching every family in the country. We'd had close encounters before, with my dad being shot at while driving his car (thankfully, the car was armored), my cousin being briefly kidnapped as he walked from his car to a friend's house, but the close encounters with these Venezuelan realities had never been fatal, every time our family had managed to remain whole, except this time. But this was not rare among friends, and acquaintances, everyone we knew had experienced a friend or family member getting kidnapped, or killed; we just didn't think it would one day be our turn.

In 2005, the indie film *Secuestro Express* was released in theaters. It was directed and written by Venezuelan Jonathan Jakubowicz. "Secuestro," meaning kidnapping in Spanish, was in fact slowly but reluctantly being accepted as a possibility for every Venezuelan, regardless of socioeconomic class. The film showcased the kidnapping style that comprised around 80% of Venezuela's kidnappings, even if most of the cases were going unreported. Who were the criminals? People who looked to make ends meet by kidnapping someone of perceived wealth for 24 hours and then return them to their life. During a typical "express" kidnapping — a practice believed to have been imported from Mexico — they take the victim and ride around the city with them to extract money from various ATMs with the victim's card, then after 8 to 24 hours, they leave the victim stranded and take their car. Of course, the film humanizes the kidnappers; it shows us how many of them have families at home. It shows one of the kidnappers talk to his daughter and comfort her; it shows us another captor arguing with his mother over the phone about what to feed the dog. It shows us that these dark crimes are coming from everyday people but also showed how a situation can go wrong.

I remember when this film was in theaters, friends that had gone to see it had such a visceral reaction to the film that some dropped to their knees as they exited the theater and cried. Today, such a reaction seems extreme, even to me. I think the reason why that was happening then was that we didn't look at the film as something that was far from us, but something that could happen to us, our friends, or family at any moment. We knew that, but we hadn't yet accepted it. The film was reality, and it was forcing us to wake up.

I had heard these declarations from friends, but I didn't dare watch the film until years later. When I did, I was already abroad. When I watched it, it wasn't shocking; in fact, it was mild. I had already come to accept that kidnapping, murder, and extortion were an everyday reality and a daily possibility. Since the film was released, more shocking things had happened, which almost made many Venezuelans too cynical. Sometimes in family gatherings, between hugs and bites of food, someone would joke about being kidnapped. Another would joke and brag about their worth, that whoever was worth more would be kidnapped first. Jokes, and jokes, and jokes. The jokes were there for comedic relief, something Venezuelans are generally good at. Still, the jokes masked a sense of astonishment as well. We often wondered how this had become our everyday life.

Those who were willing to make the investment would make sure to drive around in an armored car. Private university campuses were full of such vehicles. If you were in the middle class or above, chances are you would think of securing your car. We became well versed in driving for safety, taking different routes to school or work. We would look over our shoulder to make sure no car was following, but sometimes that wasn't enough. Some businesses, neighbors, and groups of friends held kidnap kitties, putting money aside just in case a friend or relative was taken.

Some people in the upper classes chose to take it a step further and hire escorts and bodyguards. Others would avoid this because they believed it drew too much attention. We would avoid wearing jewelry, and of course, luxury cars started collecting dust in people's garages. I vividly remember that every time we would step outside a building at night, the clock began ticking; the goal was to get into your car as quickly as possible. Regardless, the safety measures had been integrated so well into most of our lives that they became second nature, and we went on with our lives, almost forgetting we were taking those measures. It took sometimes going to other places that weren't riddled with crime to realize how different life could be.

Not too long ago, a friend of my parents, a banker in Caracas, was kidnapped and held captive for 11 months. After the fact, he was interviewed by a newspaper, and he arrived at the interview with escorts, who waited for him until he was ready to leave. In the interview, he recounted that he never saw those who took him, but he sensed that they felt a certain kind of pride when it came to their job, their "craft," which was abduction. He described how these criminals locked him in an empty room and would pass notes to ask him questions. Questions such as "How much are you worth?" In those 11 months, he only had a Bible for company, which he turned to in his time of solitude. Fortunately, he was insured for 2 million dollars for the specific circumstance of kidnapping and was able to get away. Nowadays, he just says that even though he is "free," he isn't really. He goes everywhere accompanied by bodyguards and feels that he only exchanged one state of captivity for another. He does recognize that even though he is lucky, he travels abroad when he can, just to walk freely on the streets of a foreign nation. He says he doesn't travel for tourism anymore, or to see beautiful things, but simply to walk for hours, feeling free. Despite that, he is lucky.

And he is right. Kidnappers may feel a sense of pride in their work, in their "craft." Years ago, a Spanish reporter managed to interview a man who considered kidnapping to be his career. The man said he used to be a police officer but that his salary was simply not enough to support his family. He recounted that when looking for something different, his first intention wasn't to engage in criminal activity and that at first, when he found the life, he was hesitant, but that he has outgrown that hesitancy. He says he even takes pride in his methods. He also reveals that he believes those who are higher up the chain in the kidnapping enterprise reach as far up as the Venezuelan government and that a lot of the money paid as ransom ends up in the hands of the Venezuelan government and Maduro.

I was in the 8th grade when I was told three brothers and their driver had been kidnapped on their way to school. They were taken three days after my 15th birthday. The boys belonged to a Catholic School in Caracas and came from an upper-middle-class immigrant family from Lebanon. They were Bryan, Kevin, and Jason Fadoul, aged 12, 14, and 17. It was February 23rd, 2007, when they left their home and were stopped by what they thought to be police at a checkpoint. Then their parents got the call. A few days later, the whole country knew and was demanding the return of the boys. Days went by, and we carried on with our activities, with our day-to-day lives. My brothers and I went to school, driven by my parents, we got together with friends, we went to the movies… and that family was trying to figure out a way to meet the pricey demand from the criminals to get their children back.

On the 38th day, the news broke. The brothers had been found dead in a common grave. All of them wearing their high school uniform from Nuestra Señora del Valle (Our Lady of the Valley).

A few days later, my school held a mass to honor the boys, and it was on that day that we all felt a personal tie to the family. The priest told us the news again and asked us to pray for them and the country. Then a nun read to us the letter the boys' mother had sent to the kidnappers. As she was reading, I looked around the chapel and noticed the tears streaming down every student's face.

The mother had begged the men to give her sons back to her, but she also asked if they meant to kill them, to please do it in their sleep. That was difficult to listen to, especially when they told us the criminals had dishonored the mother's wishes and shot the brothers as each other watched. At the chapel, we were confronted with what was truly wrong in our society. We understood then the kinds of people that walked among us. This was such a public case that even the government made public declarations as they condemned the acts. The truth was, their actions in government had directly or indirectly led to the dark place we found ourselves in as a nation. President Chávez called the boys' mother to console her. Then, later, on national TV, he is remembered by saying to the mother, "Quit the whining and let those boys rest in peace" (Spanish: "Deje la lloriqueadera y deje que esos muchachos descansen en paz"). That was our leader.

Every four hours, a Venezuelan is murdered. My city suddenly became one of the most unsafe places in the world. I barely knew any different. Statistics make it seem as if Venezuela is plunged into a civil war when we are in apparent times of peace. Official statistics indicated that the number of kidnappings grew over 20 times in the first 12 years of Chávez's presidency. According to some Venezuelan criminologists, at least 70% of kidnappings in the country are not reported. A field investigation carried out by InSightCrime.org in 2010 indicated that just in my city of Caracas, there are between 20 and 40 kidnappings per day. The Venezuelan Violence Observatory puts violent deaths in Venezuela as 90 out of every 100,000 inhabitants. It was and is an epidemic.

It's hard to know the actual numbers, but it is estimated that it could be much higher for all kinds of crime. A report by the Spanish newspaper *El Mundo* claimed that the police favor the investigations of crimes for families that do not inform the press. Basically, they divert the victims' families and offer them ways to "speed up procedures and assistance so as to not give information to the press in exchange for their collaboration." But how did we get here? Was it Chavista policies? Some people will disagree and say the murder and kidnapping rates were on the rise since the 1990s. However, given the big jump upwards after Chávez's election when a new crime wave started, one has to wonder. In a country with an over 90% impunity rate, who can be surprised when criminals roam free and cheat the law without consequence?

English journalist James Brabazon declared in 2014 that kidnapping crimes had skyrocketed since the late Venezuelan president came to power and that this had been partly a result of Chávez releasing thousands of violent prisoners as part of controversial reforms in the criminal justice system. Add that to the Colombian organized crime that was making its way across our border into Venezuelan territory, and the potential for crime was explosive. Brabazon also noted that criminals felt that the Venezuelan government did not care for the middle and upper classes, which gave those delinquents a sense of impunity and thought that they could get away with crimes when targeting private citizens within those social classes. His observation is acute, and Chávez did indeed make his rhetoric very hostile towards Venezuelans of wealth. This seemed initially only to be against the upper classes; however, it quickly became apparent that his contempt extended to middle-class Venezuelans as well. Especially if they disagreed with him. His rhetoric of love for the poor always remained; he loved his people just as long as they stayed poor. However, even though young middle-class men were the most targeted, the poor also lived in constant fear because they lived next door to the murderers. To take it even further, criminals that belong to criminal abduction gangs are sometimes fearful of other criminal gangs who could take them over.

Other international observers have also taken note of Venezuela's violence. Gareth A. Jones and Denis Rodgers wrote in their research book titled *Youth Violence and Latin America: An Overview and Agenda for Research*, that with the change of the political regime in 1999 and the beginning of the Bolivarian revolution, a period of transformation and political conflict began, marked by a new increase in the number and rate of violent deaths. In just the first four years of the so-called Bolivarian revolution, the murder rate had doubled in the country.

All of this violence touched everyone and continues to do so. In the early years, members of my extended family had some close calls. People were followed, threats were uttered, and my cousin was snatched for a few minutes while arriving at a birthday party. As he was getting out of his car, he was taken, but his friends, seeing the abduction take place, followed the criminals' vehicle, forcing them to release him. My father had someone shoot up his car, my mother had two men try to snatch her while she was getting to the house; fortunately, she noticed and drove off. The rising crime did eventually get my uncle. Walking his dog on a Saturday morning, his life was taken from us. Do we expect justice? No. At least not the kind of justice that can come from a flawed bureaucracy.

Violence that fights "fascists."

We have talked about the violence and insecurity that has plagued Venezuela for over two decades, worsening since the election of Chávez. As we have indicated, his interest was not in solving the crime problem facing the country, but of transforming the nation ideologically. We know that fighting crime ranked low on his plans for the nation. However, it wasn't merely that Chávez ignored crime, but that many corrupt government officials were allegedly receiving kickbacks from kidnappings and the extortion of the citizens. There were also the groups who were outright acting on their own perception for "the people" and for the interests of the "revolution" which Chávez had started. These groups are the "colectivos." The UN has, in fact, described them as paramilitary groups loyal to the Venezuelan regime. These groups generally wear dark clothing and dark masks to cover their faces.

The late Hugo Chávez used to call the opposition "fascist," as does the current puppet leader, Nicolas Maduro. The opposition politicians were "fascists" in their opinion, but civilians aligned with the opposition fit that description as well. It then follows that me, my family, and virtually most of my friends are fascists, according to the "Chavista" government. It was here where I learned the power of words, how they can quickly lose their true meaning when used in this form of deception. Regardless, the adjective was used, and therefore it justified a violent response towards those who fell under that category. The natural result was that militia groups, who believed it was their mission to defend the "revolution" at all costs, felt comfortable in reacting violently against opposition rallies. For years, the colectivos have served as an unofficial parallel force to confront demonstrators with impunity. This is why Venezuela's opposition fears the colectivos far more than they would fear a corrupt police force; because the colectivos are not officially government-sponsored, therefore they can serve as a repressive government arm without having Chávez or Maduro get their hands dirty.

Nicolas Maduro has called the colectivos in the past the "Angels of Socialism." If you were wondering how we know the Chavista government stands behind these groups, it's because they have made it very clear. There have been many situations where the opposition gathers peacefully under the protection of the Venezuelan Constitution, and masked and armed civilians appear in order to disrupt their gatherings. Sometimes these disruptions are simply caused by their appearance. Other times, they throw tear gas to create panic and disperse those who have gathered. And other times, they fire live ammo.

They have reached the point of impunity because the government is unofficially behind them. Many of the members of different groups within the colectivos don't even bother to cover their faces anymore. They see themselves as protectors of the "cause;" of keeping social order on behalf of what Chávez started: his revolution, what he used to call "La Revolución Bonita" (The Beautiful Revolution). Maduro, other than calling them "Angels of Socialism," has said on numerous occasions that he admires them; that they are an organization for the good of the community. He has said that "the colectivos work for society, for the sick, for peace, and against crime. They have been around for over 20 years as a form of organization for the people." Neither Nicolas Maduro nor the Venezuelan government have ever answered the questions which have been asked of them about how the colectivos manage to obtain tear gas, seemingly so easily — as they use it often as a tactic — given that tear gas is supposedly only issued to riot police and National Guardsmen, or why many of the colectivo members carry weapons exclusively issued for security forces. How coincidental.

Out of all the problems born during the Chavista government, the colectivos were not among them. Despite their favor under Chávez's government, the colectivos actually arose in the late 1950s and early 1960s in Venezuela. They were formed in working-class and poor neighborhoods throughout the country by leftist rebel groups inspired by the Cuban revolution. Their goal: fighting for "social justice." Groups like the so-called "Tupamaros" used to rob banks and steal cars to finance their organizations. In those days, however, although dangerous, they were mostly a nuisance for past governments and were, for the most part, persecuted by the police. By the time Chávez was elected in 1999, these groups simply aligned themselves with him informally. They gave up their idea of an armed insurrection, as they saw the man who had attempted a coup against the "powers that be" in 1992 as their natural ally.

Yes, as mentioned, Chávez encouraged these groups throughout his time in office. It is common knowledge by many Venezuelans that these groups were even subsidized and given weapons because, to Chávez, they were the guardians of the revolution. There is another misconception about the members of these groups, and it is that they all form part of armed factions, but in reality, there are people who consider themselves as part of the colectivos who actually do not form part of the armed militias, although they are the most visible arm. Some of these people do their part in a more peaceful manner, and that is social activism. They work their "social justice" magic differently. One way is through activist radio shows, where the "people's power" and equality among all people are typical subjects. However, the side which raises the most questions among the opposition and the international community are the armed colectivos, the so-called "defenders of the revolution." These "defenders," or how we should actually call them, armed thugs, keep active by carrying out extrajudicial killings, kidnappings, running extortion networks, and controlling lucrative food distribution networks in poor communities. They also traffic petrol and drugs along the Colombian border. Not exactly your typical stand-up citizens! But again, they are the "angels of socialism," so they can count on the government's protection.

Valentín Santana is one of such men of arms, a leader in the colectivo "La Piedrita," arguably one of Caracas's largest and most powerful groups. Santana is one of the most dangerous leaders, and he also has multiple arrest warrants against him for murder and attempted murder; however, he is essentially untouchable. He knows this as he walks through the city unmasked, visible, and free. When Juan Guaidó appeared on the scene in 2019 and made appeals to the military to join his cause as interim president, thereby questioning Nicolas Maduro's legitimacy as president-elect, Santana took to Twitter to post a call to his followers. He made a video, rifle in hand, calling for people to defend "the rev-olution." The next day, a paramilitary group fired live rounds at demonstrators, straight from a government building in Altamira, an opposition stronghold. To no avail, the state police attempted to confront the criminals, and what was the result of their attempt at following the law? The police chief, who ordered the operatives to detain the criminals, was dismissed the next day for interfering with the gunmen.

In February 2019, opposition groups were attempting to bring in supplies such as food and medicine from the Colombian bor-der, but the Venezuelan National Guard had been ordered by Ma-duro's government to prevent the aid from coming in. The Guards were blocking around 600 opposition members, but the group was determined and kept pushing to get in, despite the tear gas and rubber bullets. It was nothing they hadn't grown accustomed to through the years of the "Chavista" regime. Eventually, at a standstill, and with the obstinate opposition, the National Guard was ordered to step aside. At this point, this might seem like a victory for the opposition group attempting to bring in humani-tarian aid despite the government's obstruction. However, when the Guard stepped aside, the colectivos, with their covered faces, guns, and motorcycles, appeared to take their place. That's when the opposition group started running. As an official government group, the National Guard was firing rubber bullets and tear gas but the masked men were fired live ammo into the crowd. The situation went on for two hours as people hid, dragged bodies through the streets, and abandoned their attempts at bringing in the food and medicine. There is no official count of how many were wounded or killed. As expected, some government officials claimed that the opposition was lying, that the government had nothing to do with the incident. Simultaneously, Maduro came to their defense and said that if there were ever a time when there was a perceived threat to him being in office, the colectivos would come out and defend the "revolution" from every corner.

It is not difficult to look at the historical parallels between groups like the colectivos and other subversive groups which have been used in other communist uprisings. Communists and Marxists have always used these types of groups to do their dirty work for them. In the 1960s in Venezuela, they were simply a nuisance, but left unchecked, they can become a real danger, even more so when the government favors them for ideological purposes and keeps the public in line in conformity with the political plan of the governmental leader. That's what these groups are. Socialist uprisings have a mob of radicals that instills fear in the population to make them fall into place.

IX

The Relationship with the Church

I grew up Catholic, and so did everyone I know back in Caracas. I went to an Opus Dei School up until the 6th grade when I transferred to a Jesuit school because it was closer to our new home in the city. My Opus Dei school was so strict when it came to doctrine that before they admitted anyone, they went through an intensive interview process with the parents to ensure the prospective student came from a healthy family and the parents had a strong marriage. There was a firm belief in the school that the best students would come from such families, and they wanted to maintain that community strength. That was the case when I was admitted, and it was the case when my mother was admitted years before me. To me, Christianity was Catholic. I didn't come across anyone with any other religious beliefs. I didn't know anyone whose parents were divorced until I transferred to the Jesuit school, which, while still Catholic, had a more liberal policy for the students. Regardless of that, the instances of broken families were incredibly rare, and I did not come to accept it as normal until I left Venezuela and got to know the more secular world, where many of my friend's parents were divorced, and many of them had a family member with an alcohol problem. I didn't connect the dots regarding strong religious values, a strong family, and subsequently a strong society until much later when I noticed the common theme of attacking these institutions to introduce a tyrannical nanny state, coupled by a depraved and weak society.

In Venezuela, Roman Catholicism is the most widely practiced religious belief; some metrics put Catholics at 71% of the country and others at 92%. The religion was introduced during the colonial era. The Church didn't wield a great deal of political influence, but it did play a major role in education. However, this is not to say that religious beliefs and Christianity thrived; many of those who considered themselves Catholic were merely nominal Catholics and nominal Christians, simply using doctrine as nothing more than something to plan holidays around and as a utilitarian social construct but not a true belief. I believe this problem extends far beyond nominal Catholics in Venezuela. It has spread throughout our world and has allowed most of us to be complacent and comfortable in the slow degenerative nature of secularism.

Nevertheless, the Catholic Church still served as a deterrent for accepting destructive behaviors that have clearly become an issue in places like the United States and Europe. It served as a structure to keep families together and strong, and therefore it was to be attacked. However, there were other religious doctrines in Venezuela, with Protestantism being the second strongest, most likely influenced by the Scandinavian immigration to the country in the twentieth century.

When Chávez came to office, he took over numerous public schools, many of which were Catholic, and removed all religious education, regardless of the Constitution supposedly guaranteeing freedom of religion. Catholic schools would become one of the most consistent challengers to Chávez's ideologies. For example, they led the opposition and vehemently resisted the president's attempt to reform the education system in 2001. Chávez pretended many times to be a Christian while simultaneously bringing in witches who performed Santeria rituals all over the country; rumors say that some sacrificial rituals even took place at the presidential palace. I remember year by year, it became more and more common to see people walking around Caracas wearing the typical Santeria outfit, which consisted of an all-white ensemble with some pieces of jewelry.

Chávez gave preferential treatment to religious groups who kept to his ideological line. The Evangelical Council of Venezuela and representatives of the Catholic Church reported this preferential treatment. They insisted there was a privileged treatment of those groups who were friendly to the government's policies. The Catholic Church in Venezuela also condemned social media and press attacks on members of the clergy by pro-government sympathizers and cases of vandalism of church property. Church leaders perceived as politically active would note that their organizations would be sidelined because of that perception. For example, some religious groups appearing as pro-opposition would be excluded from government-organized events that were supposed to help communities, and they would be disregarded by government-run media. Chávez once accused Church leaders, saying that they are not "walking the way of God" as he accused them of supporting the Venezuelan opposition. Cardinal Velasco, a prominent prelate of the Venezuelan Catholic Church who served as the Archbishop of Caracas until his death in 2003, participated in the controversial 2002 insurrection, which led to Chávez's 47-hour resignation. President Chávez spoke directly to Cardinal Velasco and said, "It's you, Cardinal Velasco, who is assuming political stances. Check your conscience, go and step in front of God and pray an Our Father, or 20 Our Fathers and 20 Hail Marys." After Velasco's death, Chávez polemically said that Cardinal Velasco was burning in hell.

But when did this fight start? Essentially, the dispute between the Venezuelan Church and President Hugo Chávez started early in 2002, after Chávez attempted his educational reform for the first time; and when the Catholic leaders expressed their concerns at some of Chávez's remarks that said that the Church stood in the way of his revolutionary project. Then, most controversially, leaders, including the Archbishop, took part in the so-called 2002 "coup." It was not long before the Churches were being vandalized and religious statues were being defaced all over the country, but mostly in the capital city. Not long before, the late president

Chávez had described the Church as a tumor — the irony of him dying of cancer is not lost here.

The standoff between the Church and the Chavista regime did not die with Chávez, however, the opposition within the Church only became more pronounced. In fact, the Church in Venezuela has remained consistent with its criticism against the regime. Not to mention that it has denounced gravesite desecration and continuous attacks against them and the clergy. In 2016, media outlets reported that pro-government sympathizers in the state of Merida assaulted four young Catholic seminary students, accusing them of participating in an opposition rally. The assailants took their clothing and forced them to run naked through the streets. It might be that the Catholic Church has not garnered the most impeccable reputation in the last few years when it comes to the stories that have come out of the Vatican. The Church in Venezuela, however, has remained strong when confronting the government and remains one of the most trusted Venezuelan institutions. The Church remained strong while proclaiming Maduro to be an illegitimate leader, a sentiment echoed across the world by various governments, but not mirrored by the Vatican or Pope Francis, making it clear that perhaps the Venezuelan Catholic Church and the Vatican are not in lockstep. However, in Venezuela, the Church is the most unified institution among the dissenting voices of the opposition. Lawyer and columnist Thays Peñalver said that the Catholic Church in Venezuela has taken a strong stance while disregarding the systemic attacks they may suffer because of such a view. She has said that the Church speaks about murder and human rights violations that even opposition politicians have not dared to touch.

The Dean of Andrés Bello Catholic University (UCAB), one of the most prominent universities in the country, Francisco José Virtuoso, assured that "the Catholic Church in Venezuela is committed to a profound change of the Venezuelan reality, an integral social change because it is about rebuilding society in all areas of life. A change is sought that occurs with the active participation of citizens through democratic methods."

The bishops have also closed ranks in the face of threats from the supposed President Nicolas Maduro. His threats? To apply Hate Speech Laws against them and the rest of the clergy. According to Maduro and the pro-government group, the clergy's crime is that they sow discord and seek confrontation in their homilies, which often reference the hardships the country is experiencing. The Hate Laws are vague and a blatant excuse to censor speech that the government does not want to be heard, instead of their alleged purpose of keeping people safe from information that might cause them harm. The Episcopal Conference of Venezuela reacted unanimously to the vague speech law by remarking that "the Law against Hate and Intolerance is designed to criminalize anyone who causes discomfort to the government and its postulates." A political science professor and consultant also weighs in on the law and says that "the Hate Law shows how Maduro is willing to do anything, whether it be to kill an opponent or imprison a priest," and that "the bishops are in the spotlight."

A member of the Barquisimeto clergy, the fourth largest city in Venezuela, Monsignor Basabe, alluded that "the plague of political corruption has led Venezuela into moral, economic, and social ruin." And that "if anyone had to leave, it was whoever was responsible for the mess in which we have been driven to," when speaking about the millions of Venezuelans who had chosen to leave the nation in search for a better life. Maduro, on the other hand, says that in Venezuela, "everything tied to the Catholic Church is contaminated, poisoned by a counter-revolutionary vision and constant conspiracy."

It would be negligent on my part to ignore the fact that the Catholic Church has had its major scandals, some in the United States and some in the Vatican. The Church has had its controversies and controversial popes. In Venezuela, however, it has long remained steady, unified, and faithful to Church doctrine. It is still one of the most trusted institutions in the country, with over 70% of Venezuelans saying they approve of the Church. Perhaps because they have steered clear of corruption scandals sweeping through the Church in other nations, the Venezuelan Church has retained its moral authority.

The Catholic Church in Venezuela remains strong. Despite the attacks on it and threats by the government, it has remained calm. The Venezuelan archbishops have openly stated that they do not fear the threats against them for speaking the word of God and that the clergy will keep doing their work, declaring that they only work for God and the well-being of the country and not for the government. The Church, despite everything, remains a beacon of hope in a ruined nation.

X

"Freedom" of the Press

It was a Sunday evening, and that night I had decided to disregard my usual routine of going to bed early — given that I had school early in the morning — and stayed up to watch the conclusion of what had been a fight for the freedom of the press that had lasted for days, if not longer. In 2002, the oldest private TV network in Venezuela had decided to show part of the story of the 2002 protests that Chávez had wanted to conceal from public eyes. The April 2002 protests turned violent against the opposition at the hands of pro-Chávez militias, and the country was able to see it live through the numerous networks. So, Chávez stepped in and started one of his famous "Cadenas" or "chains," where he would take over the broadcasting signal of all Venezuelan networks and speak directly to the nation, thereby interrupting programming by the networks. RCTV, contrary to Chávez's efforts, decided to split the screen in two. As we watched Chávez speak calmly on one side of the screen, we saw the total chaos erupting in the streets of Caracas. It became apparent to anyone watching that Chávez was attempting to hide the situation. By doing this, RCTV then became the target of the famous "Chavismo." Chávez labeled them "fascists" and "golpistas," a difficult-to-translate term basically meaning traitors to the nation that were compliant in a coup d'état, or "insurrectionists." It was ironic that Chávez should say so, given that the most violent coup attempt in the last half-century in Venezuela was his own in 1992. A few years after this open display of challenges to the president's wishes, Chávez decided he would no longer renew RCTV's concession to broadcast on Venezuelan airwaves. On that December day, he announced that "There will be no concession for that insurrectionist television channel called Radio Caracas Television. The concession is over; the measure has already been drawn up, so get ready, turn off the equipment. No television channel that is in the service of the coup, against the people, against the nation, against national independence, will be tolerated here. Venezuela is to be respected." His decision was made in December 2006 and then reinforced by his Supreme Court, which by that time was primarily controlled by staunch Chávez loyalists.

The pronouncement was challenged by RCTV, but to no avail. The network was to lose its broadcasting license on the 27 of May 2007. Throughout the whole month of May, there were demonstrations all around the country against this governmental decision, culminating in violence and confrontations after the channel officially lost its signal. What had happened to Chávez's campaign promise, where he said that he would defend the freedom of the press? It seemed that now he was making all kinds of excuses as to why this network deserved to be shut down. Many of his supporters resorted to mental gymnastics to support his decision and still to this day boldly say that there was no effort to undermine the free press. The late evening of the 27th of May was the night when many of my peers grasped how real the threat to our democracy was. However, many naively still believed then that the solution to getting out of this subversion was democratic and political. Some still hoped that strong grassroots efforts and voting would remove these anti-democratic figures who had managed to subjugate us.

I remember watching that night. I had tuned in out of a sense of disbelief. Would they really dare take away RCTV from us? Despite the fact that I still preferred watching the CW at the time, RCTV was still symbolic of Venezuelan progress, of the golden years, which had been the 1950s. It was the oldest Venezuelan TV network. We all felt a sense of home in RCTV. The idea that they would be pushed off the air simply seemed like an illusion, as if it was not really happening. Maybe it was more like a nightmare. That day, the Venezuelan network had decided to go with special programming, showcasing the best and most successful shows they had made since the 1950s. Of course, there was an air of nostalgia, even among my peers who were too young to grasp the significance of this channel. I watched the last hour intently; the crew, the actors, the writers, the producers, and TV execs of RCTV gathered in their studio, sharing tears with their audience, promising us they would soon be back and would meet us again "in democracy." Thinking back to that moment, I remember how unreal it felt. It was as if those of us who still weren't aware that Venezuela was falling from its privileged position of freedom among other Latin American nations suddenly woke up. People who had remained apolitical up until that time and had relegated themselves to living their day-to-day lives and watching their "telenovelas" were now forced to choose a side. The whole crew on the TV screen cried to say goodbye to its faithful audience, and it was impossible not to shed a tear with them as I watched. At 11:59 pm that evening, as they concluded the singing of the National Anthem, the signal went dark, and RCTV lost its place after 53 years on channel 2. A few seconds later, a new signal reemerged: TeVes, Chávez's new TV network.

Chávez and his people said that the TV frequency would pass to the hands of the public — that from now on, it would be a utilitarian TV network at the service of the people. In reality, it became a propaganda machine in favor of his government and his ideology. The owner of 1BC, the group that owned RCTV, Marcel Granier, qualified the government's decision as "arbitrary and illegal." During the goodbye message from the network, Granier read a farewell statement in which he reiterated that the non-renewal of the license was "political revenge" and an act of discrimination in comparison to other channels where concessions had been renewed. He even suggested that their competitor, Vene-vision, owned by the magnate Gustavo Cisneros, received privi-leged treatment from the government days prior when their li-cense was renewed, despite engaging in similar tactics to RCTV in 2002. Which put into some people's minds that perhaps there were backroom deals made between Venevision and the govern-ment. Some people suggested that Venevision remained as a "controlled" opposition. However, this is all speculation. Granier also said that the decision to refuse his network's renewal was dictated by fear and "sustained by the abuse of power that is the main source of evil."

I went to sleep after watching TeVes take over the signal, which just minutes before had belonged to RCTV. I couldn't believe it. Yes, I certainly grew up watching with a child's eyes what was being done to the country, but this was the first time it really hit me. The first time all I had been warned about in history lessons was coming to fruition. The next day, the front page of one of the most prominent center-right newspapers had a headline "With protests, RCTV went off the air." That Monday morning, I showed up at school and there was a shift that had happened among my classmates as well. We had all grown up watching our parents fear the incoming authoritarianism, but now it almost felt as if the responsibility was being passed onto us. It was soon going to be our turn to start resisting the tyranny and carrying on the torch. It was soon going to be the high school students and the university students calling out the government for its trespasses. This would

certainly happen later on during student movements, which resulted in some successes, and some unfortunate deaths, as during
the student protests of 2014. RCTV spent more than half a century
sharing moments with its audience — soap operas, news, and
comedy shows which marked a chapter in the dramatic history of
the country and were a reference to the region's TV industry, with
opinion programs open to all political tendencies, and entertainment shows that captivated Venezuelan viewers. Many of those
who worked at the network left the country soon after, sparking
another wave of emigration, and hundreds without such options
were left without jobs. However, a phrase kept them united — the
slogan "we'll meet again in democracy," which many still remember to this day. The fading out of the signal of that network was
definitely a metaphorical slap in the face to many of us, but it was
also symbolic of what was to come. Years later, there have been
many more attacks against freedom of expression, although they
have not been quite as overt.

What has become of the Venezuelan press? Many will argue
that there are plenty of journalists and outlets in Venezuela that
are critical of the government. If that is the case, how can anyone
say there is no free press? The answer is simple, the opposition is
allowed to operate to a certain extent. There is a line that is not to
be crossed. Debate and the illusion of real opposition are encouraged, but the concerns of citizens are usually ignored. There is
conversation to quell the frustration of the people but no real so-

lutions. The dissenting press provides an outlet for those frustrations, giving citizens the illusion that there is no censorship and that they still have a voice. Perhaps they do, in some sense. There are undoubtedly honest journalists, and many of them continuously risk their safety, but they operate within limited confines.

A few years ago, I got an internship in a small Venezuelan news company operating out of Miami. We primarily covered Venezuelan news during 2014, a contentious year where many students took to the streets for months demanding Nicolas Maduro's resignation. I worked mainly as a staff writer, occasionally filling in for the social media person on their evening broadcast. One day, I decided to contact a political commentator for an interview — a man who, by U.S. standards, would be considered center-right. After I set up the interview with him, the general manager silently blocked it. Days went by, and I quietly inquired about it to one of my superiors. She told me that manager had deemed the interview too controversial, and that he did not want extreme right-wing views aired on the program. That was a real eye-opener for me, as I truly started to understand how things actually worked with the dissenting press. Carlos Correa, director of the non-governmental organization "Public Space," dedicated to documenting cases of censorship, said in an interview with BBC World that the "mechanisms" present do not allow people to say that there is no freedom of expression, but neither is there "full freedom." He goes on to say that there are mechanisms that are affecting the entire exercise of journalism.

During the Chavista regime, reports of attacks against journalists and media organizations by government sympathizers, who attempt to shut down any criticism of the administration, increased. Journalists are operating in a precarious environment because many of them are physically threatened when they cross a specific line, therefore creating extreme caution among journalists who genuinely want to do their jobs. They are also fined and warned against "hate speech" by the government, knowing that if they are found to be engaging in said hate speech, they can be prosecuted to the full extent of the law. Laureano Márquez, a journalist who has faced fines and government threats in the past, said, "Freedom of expression is not only being able to say things but also being free to say things without being persecuted." The National Assembly passed an illegitimate hate speech law termed a "law against hatred, intolerance, and for peaceful coexistence." This sounds caring, but it comes with up to 20 years in prison, blocking of portals, and closing radio stations to those who express opinions that inconvenience the government. The vagueness of the so-called "law" results in the possibility of arbitrary applications of said law. It can be used for the disproportionate deprivation of liberty to target those whose narratives do not fit the regime's political programs.

The NGO, Journalists Without Borders, in their 2020 Freedom of the Press rankings, ranks Venezuela at 147 out of 180 countries evaluated in terms of their degree of freedom of the press, stating that since 2010, abusive arrests and defamation trials have been carried out against journalists. In August 2020, two journalists were murdered just days apart in the nation. The NGO "Public Space" (known as Espacio Público in Spanish) states that there have been at least 270 attacks against journalists and 686 violations of the right to free speech in Venezuela since the start of 2020. They added that the Covid-19 crisis, in addition to recurrent coordinated restrictions on internet access, has made it extremely difficult for independent journalists to cover the news. Reporters Without Borders has, in fact, recognized their concern for the constant decline in respect for freedom of expression in the South American nation. International reporters have been denied entry to cover news, and a German journalist was imprisoned for 4 months on Venezuelan territory. He was lucky — he was told he could face 28 years in prison. The Venezuelan National Guard has targeted and verbally abused Latin American journalists. The headquarters of *El Nacional*, one of Venezuela's leading dailies, was attacked when masked men threw a Molotov cocktail and excrement in front of the newspaper's offices. The editor of the newspaper, *Correo del Caroní*, was given a 4-year jail term for covering corruption involving a state-owned company. The National Guards have also forcibly removed journalists covering events that the government does not want seen. The instances are numerous and could encompass an entire book. The patterns are there; the most common occurrences are detentions, evictions from public spaces or institutions, attacks against journalists or anyone recording facts and disseminating information, and attacks against media outlets or teams, mostly during street demonstrations. In

2017, the year ended with 8 small news channels being forced off the air, along with 54 radio stations and 17 print-based media outlets, which stopped circulating due to lack of paper, many indefinitely. Despite all this, even the information that gets out and is printed and broadcasted only reaches a privileged portion of the population with access to news. As people have become more impoverished, their access to accurate information gets scarcer.

RCTV's departure from the national airwaves, although painful, was just the beginning. Venezuela keeps spiraling downwards in all aspects of freedom. Historic newspapers present during the ups and downs of Venezuela's political story in the twentieth century have one by one began closing their doors, and not unlike RCTV, hoping for a comeback one day, when and if the nation finds itself again in democracy.

XI

Death of Chávez — Transition to Maduro

It was the summer of 2011, and I had decided to spend the season taking classes in Boston. I wasn't exactly thrilled at the idea of spending the entire summer in Caracas because even though I missed my home and weekends with my extended family, I knew that most of the summer would be spent in a few select places in the city that felt safe. Yes, I was still planning on going back for a month or two; I just wanted to take advantage of the freedom I had in Boston and that I knew I couldn't enjoy once I got back home. For a while now, there had been rumors about Chávez's health. My mom and I had long conversations, speculating about what it could possibly be, what they were hiding, or if, in fact, the government was hiding something.

The rumor mill started off with a knee. Chávez's knee, to be specific. The Venezuelan president publicly started talking about an old knee injury that was beginning to bother him and was causing him pain in his leg. He brushed it off, saying it was from old age, and playing baseball and serving in the military. That casual behavior from Chávez regarding his pain did not stop political pundits and doctors from speculating. Social media was riddled with questions: many venturing guesses and different possibilities. The chatter was not going to stop, especially when Chávez discussed the possibility of medical intervention and subsequently disappeared from the public and political discourse for weeks. For a public figure like Chávez, it was a red flag.

Finally, there came a voice of clarity, an official representative of the government who addressed the nation. Chávez's vice president, Nicolas Maduro, went on the Venezuelan airwaves on June 11th and announced that President Chávez, aka "El Comandante," had undergone surgery. Details were not disclosed. A certain disease was not mentioned, and there were still many questions looming. Nineteen days passed, and then Chávez himself quenched some of the thirst for answers. He reappeared on the public stage, looking as skinny as he had been when he first took office in 1999, and confirmed some of the rumors. In a 15-minute speech on public television, he did his best to appear as eloquent as always to tell the public his health was suffering and that he had a tumor. However, his attitude was that it was a passing phase and that the tumor would be defeated. A tumor, which he could not bring himself to call cancer. Chávez recounted how it was his mentor, Fidel Castro, who had given him the bad news. They had found out through an emergency surgery performed in Cuba on June 11th, when it was apparent to them that the disease could no longer be hidden from the public. "El Comandante" also narrated his reaction and how he asked the Virgin Mary for intercession and prayed to Jesus that his mission on this earth wasn't over. He not only pleaded with Jesus and Mary, but he also told us he pleaded with "other" spirits.

Now, what was next? That was the question in many people's minds. Was he fit enough to fulfill the duties of president whilst he recovered? His answer: Yes. Chávez did not want to give up his position, nor did he wish to delegate his responsibilities to anyone else. Therefore, he had the Chavista majority at the National Assembly authorize him to temporarily govern from Cuba. This authorization came despite the Venezuelan Constitution, which clearly states that the authority passes to the vice president in the event of the temporary absence of the president from Venezuela. However, at this point, it shouldn't come as a surprise to anyone that the Chavista majority in the National Assembly ignored the constitution. It was fine, as long as they got what they wanted.

So, he did govern from Cuba. We would see video broadcasts of him giving orders, telling jokes, dancing... mostly presenting his cheerful self and putting a smile forward for his public. Of course, every time he could, he would repeat his slogan: "Patria, Socialismo, o Muerte! Venceremos" (Homeland, Socialism, or Death! We will Triumph). He was carving this slogan in the minds of every Venezuelan he could. Instilling his hatred of the rich, even though he was enriching himself and his family through corruption, and etching in people's minds that the U.S. was to blame for anything that went wrong with his precious revolution. His tactic was to have the public eye continuously looking at a scapegoat instead of his own corruption and inefficiencies.

After an extended stay in Cuba, he finally returned on the first of August, triumphantly declaring that he had defeated cancer. He explained that he was going through chemotherapy, the treatment the Cuban doctors had given him had worked, and that he was recovering. Some time passed; the holidays went by. It was a new year, an electoral year, in fact, when he again, in February 2012, was forced to publicly announce that his cancer had returned. Rumors exploded again on social media. Citizens congregated on the virtual public square to speculate about what type of cancer he had, which many suspected was prostate cancer. The official diagnosis had been hidden from the public for about 20 months. His cancer had returned in February, right? Well, as early as July that same year, he assured the public he was cancer-free again. This happened to be fantastic timing for his campaign since the next election was coming up. His people needed to trust that he was healthy enough to run the nation. He assured his most ardent followers that he could, in fact, run for president again. So, he did, and he won the presidency again for the 4th time. Swiftly after he won, however, he again went to Cuba to continue with chemotherapy in the fall of 2012. He didn't even attend his own inauguration. Again, there were questions, hadn't he recovered?

No, he hadn't. About a month after he had gone to Cuba, he returned to Venezuela and announced once again that his cancer had returned. This time, however, he didn't seem so confident that it was just a passing thing. This was the first time he recognized that the disease could, in fact, cost him his life. He also said if not his life, it could cost him the presidency, something he hadn't even floated to the public yet. Therefore, he passed the responsibility down to his vice president and former bodyguard, Nicolas Maduro because the possibility of him stepping down or losing his life had become very real for him and his supporters. He made it a point to tell his supporters that they should choose Nicolas Maduro as the nation's future leader in either event.

Of course, many people didn't like the idea. Not only was Nicolas Maduro a man who many considered to be inexperienced and only in his position because of the trust and friendship he and Chávez had developed, but there were others that surrounded Chávez who were ambitious and coveted the presidency. Regardless, Chávez was still alive, and the focus was on the possibility of his imminent death. Venezuelan doctors had been weighing in for a while, and at a time when the public lacked information about the health of the president, we turned to them for answers. Dr. José Rafael Marquina, a Venezuelan medical professional with a large number of followers on social media, said very forcefully that "At this time there is no remedial but palliative for the pain he is suffering. Chávez is in the terminal phase, and that is irreversible." Marquina was making an estimation based on what he was observing, even though he hadn't personally treated Chávez. Time would prove he was correct.

Others wondered that perhaps it was the aggressive campaign he had undergone right before his re-election that had cost him his health once again. More medical professionals ventured that because of Chávez's distrust for Venezuelan doctors, he had made a mistake by going to Cuba. He also believed in sorcery acts to cure his disease, but that's another story.

One of the main reasons Chávez had chosen Cuba for his treatment was also his need for privacy, and in Cuba, the Castro brothers kept a tight grip on information. His friendship with them resulted in him trusting them with his life. Venezuelan doctors, however, believed that Cuban doctors had made some critical mistakes when it came to his diagnosis and treatment that very likely would cost him his life. Chávez, however, had explored another colorful possibility as the cause of his disease: the United States. Chávez offered that perhaps the U.S. had inoculated him with the cancer because he believed they were trying to take him down. Remember how Chávez often blamed the U.S. for unfortunate events in Venezuela? Well, this was no different. He even said the United States was responsible for a wave of cancer that had stricken some Latin American heads of state, Cristina Kirschner, with thyroid cancer being one of them. After she announced her cancer, Chávez publicly shared his theory, hypothesizing that maybe the northern empire had invented a technology that could spread cancer. He said, "I am not accusing anyone. I am simply taking advantage of my freedom to reflect and air my opinions about some very strange and hard to explain goings-on."

Chávez had previously accused the CIA of sending spy bees to Venezuela. It was not uncommon for him to have shocking theories. Still, because his bizarre ideas became so commonplace in the Venezuelan political discourse, they were promptly discarded by many political opponents and news outlets. Despite his M.O. of blaming Washington for everything, Venezuela's economy remained closely tied to the U.S., and most of its imports depended on the northern country. Although not his own, another theory blamed Cuba for his death, saying that Chávez had become obsolete and unmanageable in their need to control Venezuela; therefore, the Castro brothers had discarded him.

Hugo Chávez underwent another surgery on the 11th of December 2012 in Cuba. After that, he was never again seen in public. What happened? Did he die during surgery? Not exactly. I remember that for months we were all wondering, conjecturing, guessing what had happened. Newspapers with Chávez's image would surface of him reading newspapers with current dates, but people were doubtful that the photos were real. Why won't he speak to his public if he is well enough to take photo-ops? I wondered if Chavez had died; many others did as well. The rumor mill was speculating about his death only a couple of weeks after his surgery in Cuba. There was a propaganda effort to tell us otherwise. What were we to believe? His government officials were working hard to maintain the image of "business as usual." Dozens of documents were being signed, presumably by Chávez. What was going on?

At the time, I was still in my sophomore year of college, and that Spring, me and a few friends were able to travel to Mexico for Spring Break. Any stranger I met from Latin America wanted to have a conversation with me about Chávez and his health. A huge question mark still loomed around the matter, but at this point, I was confident that Chávez had passed away, despite any official news. In fact, I had that conversation on the afternoon of March 5th, 2013, after a day at the beach when I was ready to return to my hotel room to wind down for the evening. I discussed with an Argentinean stranger the state of Chávez's health after they heard I was Venezuelan. My conviction was that he had passed away, but they were keeping it from us. As I got back to the room, I sat down in front of the television, and I turned it on. There it was, Nicolas Maduro, the vice president of Venezuela, was officially announcing that Chávez had succumbed to cancer in Caracas, Venezuela. He was 58 years old and had battled cancer for 2 years until he lost the fight.

This was an odd moment for me and for many Venezuelans. An odd moment because we had a sense of relief since the truth was finally out and because maybe, just maybe, we now had the chance to take back our country. However, someone had just died, and we understood that being relieved at someone's death was not exactly the type of people we wanted to be. In the evening, I went downstairs before heading for dinner with my friends, and I told them the news. They could see I had a positive outlook about the future, and one of them rightly asked: "Isn't it odd to be happy at someone else's passing?" I said yes, but that it's wasn't his passing that I was happy about, I wasn't dancing on his grave or mocking him as a figure, but I was thinking of all the anguish and destruction he had caused. I was thinking of him tearing the country apart, of him mocking people like me who opposed him, of him contributing to the downward spiral that was Venezuela. I was thinking that maybe, it could all change. Of course, I would come to find out that I was wrong.

Did Chávez die that day? Maybe those of us who don't think so can be called conspiracy theorists. However, doubt has definitely remained, and even prominent people from the Chavista camp have called the date of his death into question. Military captain Leamsy Salazar, who deserted to the United States, confirmed that President Chávez died in Cuba at 4am, on December 28th, 2012, from respiratory failure. Captain Leamsy Salazar wasn't some random person in the military; he was also Chávez's Chief of Security. Chávez's bodyguard confirmed the Captain's story, saying that the Venezuelan leader had died in Cuba. Luisa Ortega, Venezuela's ex-attorney general — now in exile — gave an interview where she assured us that Hugo Chávez had really died on the 28th of December, not on March 5th the following year, despite official announcements. She recounted how she got a phone call on December 28th from Diosdado Cabello, a prominent player in Chávez's inner circle and government. In the phone call, Mr. Cabello had said, "Come here, Chávez has died." If the allegations are accurate and the rumors true, why would the government hide his death from the public for over two months? One can only speculate, but perhaps it had something to do with all those official government documents that were swiftly signed in his name right after his death, and maybe his inner circle needed some time to figure out what was next. Those in charge of this public manipulation would have benefitted politically and economically from the signing of the supposedly valid mandates of the already-dead president.

Cancer did to Chávez what many opponents couldn't do for 12 years: remove a man from power who was one of the Latin American leaders who had maintained office the longest in a supposed "democracy." If he hadn't died, his last re-election, which many international observers deemed fraudulent, would have given him a way to govern the nation uninterrupted for 20 years. Chávez had inspired a left-wing revival across Latin America. When he died, he left behind a bitterly divided nation.

Many of his supporters took to the streets, grief-stricken, somehow blaming the opposition. Sometime before the announcement of his death, university students had chained themselves together, with mattresses and tents, to protest the government and the lack of transparency about the president's health. When the announcement came, supporters of Chávez, known as "Chavistas," expressed their anger and sadness by burning the mattresses and tents the students had used to spend their days in protest. They shouted: "Are you happy now?" and "Chávez is dead; you got what you wanted!"

There was such a cult of personality surrounding Chávez that the division is still strong, 8 years after his death. When he died, people journeyed to the funeral in Caracas. They waited for hours upon hours within a multitude of people, only to catch a glimpse of his casket. Some left-leaning American news outlets praised him; the *New York Times* and other outlets framing him as an amazing leader, who only sought to diminish U.S. influence in the region when the reality is that now Venezuelans are being ruled by the Cubans, the Iranians, and the Chinese. It seemed to me that some U.S. media outlets enjoyed amplifying the idea that the United States was the cause of all our troubles as if our own politicians where little angels when, in fact, our troubles mostly were caused by corrupt politicians in our own land. But even the *New York Times* acknowledged in a column that "Over nearly a decade and a half, Mr. Chávez made most major decisions and dominated all aspects of political life." Yes, he was an authoritarian leader, meaning the separation of powers did not matter. He even packed the Supreme Court early in his presidency so that they would not go against him, and they never did.

Remember how I mentioned that Chávez tried to blame his disease on the United States? That claim resurfaced again after his death. His vice-president, who assumed the presidency until elections could be held, revived the accusation, saying cancer was given to Chávez by "enemies of the State." He even went so far as to announce that he would create a "scientific commission" solely in charge of proving that Chávez was attacked and murdered. Suffice it to say, the proof never came. Because this claim was now being made by a head of state, the international medical community felt it was necessary to weigh in on the issue, which denied the possibility that his cancer was inoculated. A Peruvian oncologist, the president of the American Society of Cancer, said that it is not possible to inject cancer into someone because the body would reject it immediately without allowing it to grow. The oncologist also said that the idea that a chemical substance can cause cancer in one shot is impossible, noting that chemicals can cause cancer only after a lot of exposure for prolonged periods.

The vice president was not only wrong, but he was also claiming that he could speak to Chávez through a bird. You can understand why at this point, many people did not take leaders like him and Chávez seriously. However, Maduro lacked Chávez's charisma, which made his colorful claims look clownish. Despite the lack of charisma and intelligence, Maduro, however, had been handpicked by Chávez to become the next president. Why Maduro? There were many other more intelligent people within the Chavista circle. Diosdado Cabello, even though a snake, certainly resented that Chávez had not picked him. Maduro, however, was more manageable. It was believed that Maduro was chosen by the Castros themselves; who wanted Maduro because they wanted a puppet whom they could manipulate.

Elections still had to be held, however. Venezuela had to maintain the appearance of a democracy. That year, 2013, an election was held between Nicolas Maduro and his opponent Henrique Capriles Radonski. It was the first year that I could legally vote, and even though I was still in school in Boston, dozens of Venezuelans abroad accompanied me to the polls on Boylston Street. It was an exciting day. We knew fraud was entirely possible, but not to the level that could completely revoke the will of over 80% of the people. On the day of the election, I went to lunch with some Venezuelan friends, had some Venezuelan food that the Boston restaurant near the voting polls was graciously providing. Then we all went to gather in separate apartments throughout Boston to watch the election with our friends.

At the beginning of the night, a sense of joy and hope filled the air. Perhaps, this was the time we would finally beat the system that had been rigged against us. Our thought was: the Chavistas won't be able to garner much turnout, no matter how much they threaten people to vote for them because the charismatic leader who drove the movement was gone. The night went on, and the votes were pouring in; it seemed our side was winning by a landslide. Then suddenly, in the late evening, Tibisay Lucena, head of the National Electoral Council, came out to announce to the public that the counting of the votes had to be suspended for a time because of "technical difficulties." We knew something was wrong. They resumed shortly after, and it wasn't long after that the election results changed and they declared Nicolas Maduro to be the next president of Venezuela. As I write this, I still feel a sense of shock and anger. I remember the wave of disbelief that passed over my friends' faces who were in that room watching. Tears were shed, and the idea of never getting out of this nightmare seemed like something we just had to accept. I went back to my own apartment, had a shot of tequila, announced to my social media that I was having said shot of tequila, and proceeded to go to bed.

Maduro had won by 50.61% of the vote to Capriles' 49.12%. Even the Chavista camp was surprised it was so close. We were sure the elections were rigged, but because we had garnered so much support through the Venezuelan student movement, we almost turned the tide in our favor, despite their cheating. Henrique Capriles and the opposition requested a recount. We needed a leader to be bold and speak for us. Many Venezuelans were ready to take to the streets and shout to the world that our elections had been stolen. Capriles himself said that they had been stolen, but he encouraged us to stay calm, that all would be well. The recount never came, the electoral council rejected the request, and Capriles' voice grew silent by the day. It seemed that he had become nothing but controlled opposition, nothing but a shell to our expectations. Soon the unity within the opposition movement was disintegrating, splitting between those who wanted a strong right-wing voice that would fight for us and those who just wanted everyone in line so we could be united, and compromise with the enemy.

XII
Life in Exile

I was 15 when I heard someone had shot up my dad's car. He was supposed to pick us up from school that day, but circumstances had changed. At that point, most people who could afford it would have their car armored. Thankfully, that was the case for him as well. He had been driving home from the vet when a man on a motorcycle stopped right next to him at a red light. The man gestured to my father, pointing to his watch, to which my dad responded by mouthing the time of day, "it's 12pm," he said. The man took out his gun and knocked on the window. As it escalated with my father refusing to budge, the man pointed his gun and shot at the whole driver's side of the car before finally giving up as my father maneuvered to use the vehicle against the gunman, seeing the scene, and the possibility of my dad's car coming up against his motorcycle, the man turned around and drove off.

It was a shocking sight to see our family car covered in bullet holes. We knew that it was getting more dangerous every day in our city. We had friends of friends who had been kidnapped, while family friends and my cousin had a very close call. My father, who had always said he wanted to ride out the storm called "Chavismo," was suddenly wondering why we were still there. Why were we risking our lives?

Around that same time, I was seriously thinking about my future and my education, which seemed to be under attack in Venezuela. Going abroad for university had always been at the back of my mind; however, it was out of a spirit of adventure, of experiencing the world, always with the idea of returning to Venezuela for a career and living out the rest of my life there. I began to notice that things were changing, that the education system was again under attack. Now people felt that maybe private institutions would not be able to avoid the governmental influence. There were conversations I was hearing from parents and family who were worried about our schools. The government was imposing price controls on private schools, making it harder for them to survive without government favor and/or control. Suddenly I thought if I didn't leave right then, my future would be compromised. So, I left. I made the decision to start a new life and enroll in boarding school. Convincing my family was not difficult. People my age were being kidnapped daily, and the "express kidnappings" became all too normal. Leaving was both scary and exciting, and thankfully, my family was in a position to send me abroad.

I ended up in a small Swiss town overlooking Mont Blanc. A small village in the mountains would be my new home for the next two years. It was quite a striking change from my life in the capital city of Venezuela. It took me some time to adapt to how safe it was to walk outside the school's gates. I would sometimes wake up early in the morning to the sound of cows and the bells that hung from their necks, walking through the town's small streets.

This was where my life began to take a whole new path. I encountered people from Azerbaijan, Russia, Ghana, Kazakhstan, Germany, Spain; the list goes on. Granted, they were all people whose families could afford to send them to these schools. But my world began opening up. I was no longer in a Caracas society echo chamber. It was in this school where my views on Chávez were strongly challenged for the first time. I remember at 16, getting into an argument with a Swiss-French teacher in a class where we were discussing the European Union and its future. It was when she mentioned "socialism" and its numerous benefits that I dared disagree with her. I told her about my perceptions of this economic system and how it had failed Venezuela. As the higher authority in the room, she explained how I was simply too young to understand and how "I would see" that Chávez and his policies were actually good for the Venezuelan people. She argued that it was too early to tell at the time but that it was clear to her that Chávez and his socialist revolution would be a triumph for Venezuelans.

She was right in that I was too young to understand or argue certain things. At the time, I couldn't quite put into words how much I disagreed with her. I let her have her say, and some doubt started to creep into my mind. I wondered if I was missing something, if perhaps maybe I was the one who was mistaken. I decided to take my questions to someone I considered better informed, a higher authority on the subject: my history teacher, whose family had fled the USSR to take refuge in the U.K. I went to her to ask for her opinion on Chávez, to which she immediately replied, "Oh, he's a dictator," and walked off. Her answer was confirming my own belief at a time when the international community still viewed Chávez as a democratic, progressive leader.

I had many such encounters throughout the years when I was in Switzerland and then in Boston. Just by saying I was Venezuelan, many people would want to engage in a political discussion with me. Many of those would end in contentious arguments, from taxi drivers to professors. They all thought I just "didn't understand what Chávez was doing" and that "I would see." Time, of course, proved them wrong.

I remember seeing people like Sean Penn and Naomi Campbell going to Venezuela and getting a presidential tour with Chávez himself, not realizing they were being mouthpieces and pawns aiding in the destruction of the country. Helping to destroy the lives of millions of Venezuelans from the humblest of backgrounds. It was infuriating, to say the least. I watched as Hollywood millionaires helped the Venezuelan regime stay in good standing with the international public. How they would help spread their poisonous ideas. What for? To relieve some kind of guilt they had for their own wealth? To signal to the American public, they cared for the world over their own vanity? I still wonder this when I see Hollywood types defend the poisonous socialism.

I went to college in Boston, and throughout my college years, it seemed the world was more aware of the failed experiment that was and is Venezuelan socialism. Despite that, I did have my disagreements with professors in smaller classes, and when the topic of Venezuela wasn't mentioned, I began to open my mind to more "progressive" economic ideas. I thought maybe they were right about Democratic-Socialism in Sweden. Those ideas, of course, lasted for about 5 minutes in my mind. In 2014, protests exploded throughout my entire country. My peers who had stayed and gone to college in Caracas were out marching every day, demanding the resignation of the man many viewed as an illegitimate president: Nicolas Maduro.

Students and other citizens all over the country had halted their lives to invoke Article 350 of the Venezuelan Constitution. The article reads as follows: "The people of Venezuela, true to their republican tradition and their struggle for independence, peace and freedom, shall disown any regime, legislation, or authority that violates democratic values, principles, and guarantees or encroaches upon human rights."

It was clear to most Venezuelans at home and abroad that the current Venezuelan government was violating democratic values and abusing our Constitution. Our community stood up across the world to give symbolic support to those risking their lives on the country's streets which once were the symbol of freedom for South America. I was in my Junior Spring semester, but I was no longer preoccupied with my classes. I felt a sense of guilt if I went out with friends on the weekend when I knew my friends back home couldn't do the same at this time.

I thought the international community was fully behind us and the students. Stories were coming out daily of people being killed, imprisoned, or wounded in the protests. I went to a rally in Boston to gather with other Venezuelans and allies and send support to people back home. We couldn't be there with them, but at least we could show them they weren't alone. Many times, we were confronted by groups of American leftists. Americans who would sport Che Guevara's face on their t-shirts, who would fly the Cuban flag, who would hold up the revolutionary fist of Marxism. I tried to have conversations with these people, but they would tell me, and others who were there, about our "privilege" and our lack of understanding of our own country. They were immutable in their beliefs and would refuse to have conversations; they were just there to drown out our voices. I attributed that to ignorance, but I noticed how similar they were to the resentful minority in Venezuela that had always defended Chávez and had always professed to hate the rich.

Then came an article from *Al-Jazeera* urging the United States to side with the Venezuelan government against the students who were demanding a return to democracy. It was an article written and signed by 46 academics from all over the United States — as if their status as university professors was somehow more valid than that of the students and other hundreds of thousands of Venezuelans invoking article 350 of our Carta Magna, our Constitution. As if it was the students attacking Venezuelan democracy. This memory still brings me so much frustration that I feel like my hands will start shaking, as I write this. Thinking about the amount of opposition we have had to deal with, not only from our own murderous government and military but also from professors in universities abroad, is infuriating, to say the least.

I read this letter on *Al Jazeera* over and over. It implied that the opposition was wrong, and they implored the United States to stand by Venezuela's rule of law and its institutions. That rule of law that had been caught multiple times on camera using unnecessary force against protesters. The letter made the rounds amongst my peers, both in Venezuela and abroad. We were outraged. I read the names of those professors who had signed the letter. It had come from American professors in universities all over the world. I wrote on my Facebook page, urging my friends to see if their universities were included on the list. If they were, I urged them to email those professors on their campus. Finally, I thought, "I could easily find all of their emails; I should just do it." And so, I did, during an international affairs class where the professor was discussing the IRA. In 20 minutes, I put out a letter that would most likely fall on deaf leftist ears.

Dear Professors,

I am an International Affairs and Communication Studies double major at Northeastern University. I am also a Venezuelan student, which is why I decided to reach out to you; because the idea of keeping quiet simply did not seem like an option.

I am currently very proud to be a student at Northeastern University because I did not see any professors from my university sign their names to the letter you signed to John Kerry, urging him to respect the presidency of Nicolas Maduro. I have always admired all of the universities represented in that letter. However, at the moment, I am not the only student who doubts your allegations as a professor and even your credibility. I apologize if you feel offended, but I felt offended when I read that letter; just like thousands of Venezuelan students fighting for change, would probably feel insulted if they read it. I am not writing against your ideological views, which, even though I probably disagree with them, I respect them. I am not going to dwell on the letter's irony, which writes to a U.S. official who Elias Jaua (a Venezuelan minister) and Nicolas Maduro have called assassin on several occasions. I am not going to tell you in detail the reasons for the protest, like scarcity and a soaring crime rate, nor am

I going to respond in detail to the several fallacies the document you signed presented. I am not going to rant about the sadness and disappointment some Harvard alumni must feel at this letter because of some of the signatories from the Ivy League, most exemplary because Leopoldo López, a Harvard graduate, has been imprisoned for over a month with no trial. No, from this point forward, I am only going to talk about the law, which you so fervently claim to defend in your communication to the Secretary of State.

I have to admit, I am not a law student. I am simply a Venezuelan who knows her rights. These past few weeks, I have memorized article 350 of the Venezuelan Carta Magna, the article that millions of students are abiding by during their struggle.

The article states, "The people of Venezuela, true to their republican tradition and their struggle for independence, peace and freedom, shall disown any regime, legislation or authority that violates the values, democratic principles, and guarantees, or encroaches upon human rights." You might disagree that the students have enough reasons to believe this article should be applied, but in their view (which I share), their freedom has been violated in more ways than one. Democracy, which they defend, and you claim to defend, does not only consist of elections, nor are they even the essence for democracy. Democracy allows for freedom of speech and independent institutions within the government, which no longer seems to be the case. If you disagree, then you should evaluate what your ideas are for freedom of speech; for in Venezuela, there is not a single public news channel that informs the views from the opposition, and in these past few days, they have shown their bias by only broadcasting pro-government demonstrations and none of the massive opposition rallies. The People's defendant has justified the abuses of power coming from the National Guard. Hundreds of statements have been issued denouncing torture, and they have been dismissed and/or justified. One of the most memorable cases is of a National Guard beating a woman with her helmet while she pinned her against the floor. The woman beaten was charged, and the guard (who has been identified) has been exempt.

Article 132: "The National Armed Forces are an apolitical, obedient and non-deliberative institution, organized by the State to secure the national defense, stability of democratic institutions and respect for the Constitution and the law, whose observance is always above any other obligation. The National Armed Forces shall be at the service of the Republic, and in no case to a person or political bias." This article has been violated by the government a number of times, not only under Nicolas Maduro but also under Hugo Chávez, when they declared themselves to be "radically Chavista." To this day, the government uses the FANB (Armed forces) to portray their power by the showcase of unconstitutional pro-government marches.

Article 182: "To be elected President of the Republic, the candidate must be Venezuelan by birth, over thirty years of age and not be a member of the clergy." Nicolas Maduro has not only failed to prove his Venezuelan nationality but has dismissed valid proofs of his Colombian nationality. In addition, members of the Venezuelan government have not seemed to agree on where Mr. Maduro was born, since at least four of them have named different places of his birth in Venezuela. Walter Márquez, a Venezuelan congressman (diputado) and historian, has found that Nicolas Maduro's birth certificate is not recorded in any civil registry in Caracas, by which his identification is fraudulent. Officials have curiously declined to comment on this. He has found that Mr. Maduro has contradicted himself a number of times, especially when it comes to where his mother was born. Once he said she was born in the city of Rubio in Venezuela, when previously he had said she was born in Cucuta, Colombia.

Article 184: "A person who is in the office of President for the time of the election, or has been operating for over a hundred days in the preceding year, or who has relatives within the third degree of consanguinity or second degree in the presidency cannot be elected President of the Republic." I think this one needs no explanation. Not only did President Hugo Chávez himself violate this rule, but also Nicolas Maduro since he was president-in-charge when he ran for president.

The National Electoral Council (CNE) members, going against the law, have publicly identified to be Chavistas, including the president of the council, Tibisay Lucena, who mocks the law by constantly parading with the Chavista colors. Five permanent members, four of which identify with the Chavista movement, make up the CNE. This does not guarantee a free and fair election since they should be impartial. Also, their periods have expired, but they continue to exercise their functions with no objection from the other public institutions.

I can continue listing ways in which the government has violated the law, but I believe this email would then become too long, and I also have other obligations. If those are not enough reasons for you, I suggest you revise your idea of what the rule of law is; since the government should be the first and foremost example. Government officials should be the most obedient to the law. They are public servants and not above the law. A country is in trouble when the president talks all day and believes himself to be the most important person in the nation.

I invite you to read this post by a respected blogger. He also responded to the letter you signed; he touches on the points that I did not cover:

http://lasarmasdecoronel.blogspot.com/search?q=a+letter+to

Hopefully, you will respect the students' legitimate fight to gain back their democracy, and if you truly believe Maduro's words, then follow his advice: he does not want the "empire" or any "gringo pitiyanki" meddling in Venezuelan business. I want to make sure you know; I do not share his views on insulting sectors of the population or any international body. I respect different points of view, but I (along with my family and friends) have been called a fascist oligarch too many times by the government simply because I believe that all Venezuelans should be equal in the eyes of the law. A government that mocks and insults half of its population does not deserve my respect.

After putting together the letter, I found 46 Venezuelan students to co-sign it with me. I sent it out and even got it published on a Venezuelan political blog. It wasn't surprising when I received less than ten responses after sending it to the 46 professors; the ones who did... barely defended their position. They said something akin to "maybe they'll look into it."

The letter contradicted their formed assumptions about the leftist/socialist Venezuelan government and its "progressive" revolution; I'm sure most of them weren't willing to go through the cognitive dissonance it meant to maybe evaluate things from a different position — a different angle. For most of these professors, if not all of them, socialism was nothing but a theory that hadn't come to fruition. No matter how much the practical historical examples proved how much of a failure it was wherever it was tried. Their theory was, and is, a romantic and utopian view of the world. Most of them rejected the realities the world and the testimonies of people who had lived through the disasters that resulted from taking this idea and putting it into practice. For these leftist intellectuals, the people that voiced their rejection of that failed economic system simply weren't clever enough to understand what was good for them. It became evident to me that the rejection from these professors and academics to anything that offered a contrarian story to what they believed was deemed unsophisticated. Theirs was an elitist stance coming from a space of perceived intellectual superiority; while simultaneously unaware of their hypocrisy in advocating for a system of "equality" of outcome.

Unfortunately, to my surprise, in the time I have spent in the United States since 2010, I have seen these kinds of views steadily rise in popularity. Especially among my peers and those that followed my generation after college. Suddenly, Democratic Socialist was the new buzzword among millennials and Gen-Zers. I was shocked, but I also felt a sense of curiosity to learn why people in this country were open to socialism. It was obvious to me that socialism should always be rejected. After all, a diverse society only sustain it with a government forcing citizens into conformity. So how come it wasn't apparent to others? Democratic socialism and the rise in popularity of these ideas made me question my own. Perhaps there is something to Scandinavian-style socialism, perhaps it's about culture, perhaps it was about its ethnic homogeneity, perhaps a country that had already reached first-world status could actually go down this path and achieve something great for its citizens. I didn't realize how much I had to learn about the history of my own country. How much propaganda was being spewed to create the illusion of Scandinavian Socialism? In reality, it was all a myth. My own country was on the rise to become a first-world nation midway through the twentieth century, and it was progressive policies that inhibited its growth, it was the altruism that led to massive immigration from the poorest sectors of our neighboring nations, it was the slow trickle of socialism that limited wealth creation and eventually led to widespread corruption in the government, and a widening wealth gap, finally leading to the election of Hugo Chávez Frías. Chávez pressed the accelerator of socialism and put the nail in the coffin of a country already struggling to get back on track after the failures of progressive politicians.

After those massive protests in 2014 in Venezuela, I saw how people just got back to their lives. Getting used to the "new normal." People are incredibly resilient and adaptable. So, they adapted. Those who didn't adapt started a new wave of emigration. Venezuelans with Spanish ancestry moved quickly to ask for

Spanish citizenship; others went to Italy, claiming their Italian ancestry. Venezuela was a country of immigrants; people had moved there for the promise of a new world and a new life. But there was no longer a promise of a future. Those who were the children, grandchildren, and great-grandchildren of immigrants who had built a better life from their home countries were returning to the lands their families once left. Others that didn't have such possibilities explored neighboring countries. Others moved to what they perceived to be the "Land of Opportunity." The country they never imagined would ever entertain the idea of socialism: The United States of America.

Seeing the return to a new normal in my country, I decided it was time to stop investing my energy in hoping things would change. I stopped paying attention to the daily developments of Venezuelan politics because no matter how much something seemed like it would finally make a difference, nothing ever happened. In 2017, there was another wave of protests, and for a moment, I allowed myself to wonder... maybe this time. But that time wasn't to be, either. People again went back to the new "new normal. The leaders the people had elected to fight for them seem to be disorganized or complicit. They had no one in a position of power to fight for Venezuelans. At least it seemed that way then and seems that way now. The Narco-Venezuelan government had cemented their power in all the right places. And regardless of the plight of the Venezuelans on the streets, that was not going to change.

Once the socialist "progressive" government was elected into power, they stayed. It won't be democracy that removes a government like that. Their excuse is always fighting some outside enemy. Everything they do is for "the good of the people," regardless of the truth. "The people" are hardly better off now than they were before Chávez. In fact, quite the opposite is true.

Regardless of my wishes for my home country, I have also been living in the United States since 2010. Initially, I had a sense that American politics were somewhat boring and that that was a good thing. That meant stability. Quite the opposite from the circus I had seen growing up. These past few years, however, things have become quite different; to my surprise, I saw the rise in support for socialist ideas. How political movements have become more radical and more leftist. How propaganda has taken over the American media and how censorship reigns through social media. I started to pay attention. Not only for the sake of the United States and its Democratic and Republican principles, but there seems to be a wave of far-left and progressives sweeping across western nations — many of the nations that have been the beacons of economic and human progress throughout the world. I know that many of them will mirror what happens in the United States; whatever way the United States goes, it will ripple through the rest of the world. Whether it stays a nation of individual freedoms, or it doesn't. So far, we are watching the movie in real time.

Conclusion

Venezuela, as a country, began with a lot of promise. With a vision for its future and the future of its population very different from what we have today. Part of me thinks the country is already lost. That it is no longer the country my family immigrated to a few generations ago or the country of my grandparents who lived through its golden era in the 1950s. What they contributed was what they brought from the old continent, but those values and work ethics are simply lost in this new and unimproved version of Venezuela.

Leaving those Republican and European principles that were the foundation of the nation, even if little by little, was the beginning of the end of the downward spiral. I wrote this book with the intention of better understanding my country, but also of better understanding how we got here and how I can see similar patterns emerge in other nations.

It is true that the story of the fall of one country is not the same as another. In some nations, it happens faster, and in others, it's a slower process requiring academic indoctrination of generations of nationals. Sometimes that slow process is what guarantees the end result. Enslaving a population to its government. Having the government as your God.

Today, unfortunately, I am seeing a similar pattern emerge in North America. The country which has long been synonymous with freedom. But little by little, citizens have chosen to sacrifice those freedoms in favor of everyday conveniences and out of fear of offending someone who does not share their opinions.

The country that welcomed me has, little by little, been losing those founding principles which made it what it was. Institutions systematically attack their traditional values and push for a more Orwellian world. Little by little, the vestiges of this great nation are being lost by "liberalization."

People seem to have this strange belief that a great country is immune to falling and losing its status no matter what they do. History, however, has proven time and time again that the strongest of empires fall once people become complacent. It is easy to look at a country like Venezuela and think that it was already lost, that it never stood a chance. The destiny it has suffered, however, would never have been imagined by the European immigrants who came to the country in waves in the twentieth century after two wars destroyed their continent; or the Germans who settled a colony near the capital city in the nineteenth century, or any Venezuelan living through the 1950s.

The American President Ronald Reagan once said, "*Freedom is never more than a generation away from extinction. We didn't pass it to our children in the bloodstream. It must be fought for, protected, and handed on for them to do the same, or one day we will spend our sunset years telling our children and our children's children what it was once like in the United States where men were free."*

That applies to Venezuela and to all countries that have ever been free. Those values must always be nurtured and protected. But all of us in the West seem to have reached a point of complacency.

Venezuela is totally devastated. It is economically destroyed, and its most productive people have left the country amidst a massive brain drain, realizing that there was no real future and that their skills were looked down upon by the ruling elite. The recovery is very difficult, but not impossible. It is true that it has been through worse times, but perhaps we can see a situation like that of the rising Phoenix. The first thing that would have to happen is to remove the people who destroyed it and that people with the will to rebuild return home. There would be a lot to do, and the odds are against it. But I offer the idea that nothing is impossible for the kinds of people who are descendants of world builders, however few there may be left in the world. I offer that as some hope for those countries that also seem to be on the precipice of spiraling downwards into communism; however bleak, there is a way to turn things around, but with a lot of work, and a lot of optimism.

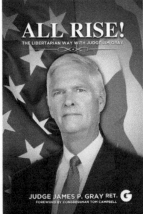
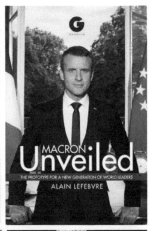

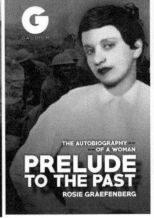

BV - #0009 - 191121 - C0 - 229/152/11 - CC - 9781592111343 - Gloss Lamination